Sir James, W. Redhouse

A simplified Grammar of the Ottoman-Turkish Language

Sir James, W. Redhouse

A simplified Grammar of the Ottoman-Turkish Language

ISBN/EAN: 9783743316119

Manufactured in Europe, USA, Canada, Australia, Japa

Cover: Foto ©ninafisch / pixelio.de

Manufactured and distributed by brebook publishing software
(www.brebook.com)

Sir James, W. Redhouse

A simplified Grammar of the Ottoman-Turkish Language

TRÜBNER'S COLLECTION

OF

SIMPLIFIED GRAMMARS

OF THE PRINCIPAL

ASIATIC AND EUROPEAN LANGUAGES.

EDITED BY

REINHOLD ROST, LL.D., PH.D.

———

IX.

OTTOMAN TURKISH.

BY J. W. REDHOUSE.

TRÜBNER'S COLLECTION OF SIMPLIFIED GRAMMARS OF THE PRINCIPAL ASIATIC AND EUROPEAN LANGUAGES.

EDITED BY REINHOLD ROST, LL.D., Ph.D.

I.
HINDUSTANI, PERSIAN, AND ARABIC.
By the late
E. H. PALMER, M.A.
Price 5s.

II.
HUNGARIAN.
By I. SINGER.
Price 4s. 6d.

III.
BASQUE.
By W. VAN EYS.
Price 3s. 6d.

IV.
MALAGASY.
By G. W. PARKER.
Price 5s.

V.
MODERN GREEK.
By E. M. GELDART, M.A.
Price 2s. 6d.

VI.
ROUMANIAN.
By R. TORCEANU.
Price 5s.

VII.
TIBETAN.
By H. A. JASCHKE.
Price 5s.

VIII.
DANISH.
By E. C. OTTÉ.
Price 3s. 6d.

IX.
OTTOMAN TURKISH.
By J. W. REDHOUSE.
Price 10s. 6d.

Grammars of the following are in preparation :—
Albanese, Anglo-Saxon, Assyrian, Bohemian, Bulgarian, Burmese, Chinese, Cymric and Gaelic, Dutch, Egyptian, Finnish, Hebrew, Kurdish, Malay, Pali, Polish, Russian, Sanskrit, Serbian, Siamese, Singhalese, Swedish, &c., &c., &c.

LONDON: TRÜBNER & CO., LUDGATE HILL.

A

SIMPLIFIED GRAMMAR

OF THE

OTTOMAN-TURKISH LANGUAGE.

BY

J. W. REDHOUSE, M.R.A.S.,

HON. MEMBER OF THE ROYAL SOCIETY OF LITERATURE

LONDON:

TRÜBNER & CO., LUDGATE HILL.

——

1884.

TABLE OF CONTENTS.

CHAPTER III.

THE OTTOMAN SYNTAX.

ERRATA.

PREFACE.

The Ottoman Language, عُثْمَانْلُوجَه ósmánlîjá, is the most highly polished branch of the great Turkish tongue, which is spoken, with dialectic variations, across the whole breadth, nearly, of the middle region of the continent of Asia, impinging into Europe, even, in the Ottoman provinces, and also, in Southern Russia, up to the frontiers of the old kingdom of Poland.

The Ottoman language is, in its grammar and vocabulary, fundamentally Turkish. It has, however, adopted, and continues more and more to adopt, as required, a vast number of Arabic, Persian, and foreign words (Greek, Armenian, Slavonic, Hungarian, Italian, French, English, &c.), together with the use of a few of the grammatical rules of the Arabic and Persian, which are given as Turkish rules in the following pages, their origin being in each case specified.

The great Turkish language, تُرْكْجَه túrkjé, Ottoman and non-Ottoman, has been classed by European writers as one of the "agglutinative" languages ; not inflecting its words, but

"glueing on," as it were, particles, "which were once independent words," to the root-words, and thus forming all
the grammatical and derivative desinences in use.

To my mind, this term "*agglutinative*," and its definition,
are inapplicable to the Turkish language in general, and to
the Ottoman Turkish in particular. These are, essentially
and most truly, inflexional tongues ; none of their inflexions
ever having been "independent words," but modifying particles only.

The distinctive character of all the Turkish languages, or
dialects, is that the root of a whole family, however numerous,
of inflexions and derivations, is always recognizable at sight,
seldom suffering any modification whatever, and always standing at the head of the inflexions or derivations, however
complex in character these may be. When a modification
of a root-word does take place, it is always of the simplest
kind, always the softening of a hard or sharp consonant into
the corresponding more liquid letter, and always of the final
consonant only of the root. Thus, a ت or ط sometimes
becomes a د, a چ becomes a غ, a sharp Arabic ك becomes a
soft Persian گ, or the Ottoman modification of this latter,
which is then pronounced like our most useful consonant *y*,
or, in case of a dominant *o* or *u* vowel in the root, is pronounced like our consonant *w*.

The Ottoman Turkish has more vowel-sounds (eleven in number) than any other tongue known to me. As each of these may have a short and a long modification, they make twenty-two possible vowels in all. Every one of these is distinguished by a special mark in the transliterations of the present treatise, though it is impossible to attempt any such differentiation in the Arabic characters to which the Ottoman language is wedded.

The rules of euphony regulate the pronunciation of every word in the Ottoman language; perfectly, in all of Turkish origin; and as far as is practicable, in what is radically foreign.

Although a compound word is a thing totally unknown to the Turkish dialects, and of very rare occurrence in Arabic, the Ottoman language abounds with such, adopted from the Aryan, compounding Persian.

Persian grammarians and writers first learnt how to mould into a harmonious whole the incongruous Aryan Persian and Semitic Arabic elements. Ottoman ingenuity has gone a step further, and blended in one noble speech the three conflicting elements of the Aryan, Semitic and Turanian classes of vocables.

Fault is found by some with this intermixture of idioms;

but an Englishman, of all the world, will know how to appre-
ciate a clever mosaic of diction; and a real student of the
language will learn to admire many a true beauty, resulting
from a masterly handling of the materials at his command,
by any first-rate Ottoman literary celebrity, whether prose-
writer or poet.

NOTE.—The manuscript of the present sketch Grammar was completed
before Christmas, 1882, and copies of my table of identic alphabets have been
in the hands of a few friends for the last four or five years. I have just
had the pleasure and privilege of reading the admirable and exhaustive
treatise on " The Alphabet," by the Rev. Isaac Taylor, and am rejoiced to
find that he has come to the same conclusion as to the identity of the
three; probably at an earlier date than the time, perhaps twenty years ago,
when the idea began to force itself on my mind. I still feel inclined,
however, to hold by the inference that the Phenicians gave the alphabet
to Italy, quite independently of the Greek action which later on doubtlessly
influenced the Italian culture.

LONDON,
September, 1883.   J. W. R.

OTTOMAN TURKISH GRAMMAR.

CHAPTER I.

THE LETTERS AND ORTHOGRAPHY.

SECTION I. *The Number, Order, Forms, and Names of the Letters.*

THERE are thirty-one distinct letters used in the Ottoman language. Some of these have more than one value; and four of them are sometimes consonants, sometimes vowels. There is also a combination of two letters into one character, لا or لا, lå, which Arabian piety has agreed to count as a letter, and which Persian and Turkish conformity has had no option but to adopt. Thirty-two letters have, therefore, to be named and enumerated, as follows :—

ا èllf, ب bè, پ pè, ت tè, ث sè, ج jìm, چ chìm, ح hå, خ khì,
د dål, ذ zèl, ر rì, ز zè, ژ zhè, س sìn, ش shìn, ص såd, ض dåd,
ط tì, ظ zì, ع 'åyn, غ gåyn, ف fè, ق qåf, ك kåf, ل låm, م mìm,
ن nùn, و wòv, ه hè, لا låm-èllf, ى yè.

The foregoing is the ordinary arrangement of the letters of the Ottoman alphabet, as learnt and repeated by children;

excepting that they are not at first taught to mention, or to know, either of the three Persian letters, پ pè, چ chím, and ژ zhé, which are not contained in the Arabic alphabet, their sounds and values being unknown to, and unpronounceable by, an Arab. It is called the élíf-bé, الف به, i.e., *the alphabet;* and it might be conveniently styled the *alphabet by forms;* letters of the same form being brought together in it, more or less.

There is another very different order necessary to be learnt of the twenty-nine Arabic letters. It is called ébjéd, أَبْجَد, and is arranged in eight conventional words, as follows :

أَبْجَد ébjéd, هَوَّز hévwàz, حُطِّي hútti, كَلَمَن kélémàn, سَعَفَص sá'fás, قَرَشَت qáráshát, نَخَذ sákház, ضَظَغلَ dázágllà.

The letters of the Arabic alphabet, as arranged in this ébjéd series, have each a numerical value. The first nine in order represent the nine units, 1 to 9; the second nine stand for the tens, also in order, 10 to 90 ; the third nine count as the hundreds, serially, 100 to 900 ; the twenty-eighth in the series, غ, stands for 1000; and the last, Ⴘ, though always enumerated, has no value of its own, but counts as the sum of the values of its two components, ل 30, ١ 1; *i. e.,* as 31.

This system appears to have been in use in very early times indeed. The order of the letters in it is that of the Hebrew alphabet, as far as this goes; that is, as far as the end of the sixth word cáráshát, قَرَشَت, with which the Hebrew alphabet terminates. The letters of the two last words (omitting now all consideration of the factitious ي) are Semitic inventions of a comparatively modern date, and are modifications, by means of dots, of letters, undotted or dotted, represented in the Hebrew alphabet. Thus, ث is modified from ت, خ is from ح, ذ from د, ض from ص, ظ from ط, and غ from ع. This may be called *the numeral alphabet.*

A circumstance that invests this èbjèd arrangement with a European antiquarian interest of the very highest order, is the fact that it proves, beyond the remotest shadow of a doubt, the unity of origin of the Semitic (usually taken to be Phenician, but I imagine it to be much more ancient than Moses, or even Abraham), the Greek, and the Latin alphabets. Not only can the now divergent forms of each separate letter in the series be traced through successive modifications back to one ancient Phenician character, but the order of the whole series from ا to ث is absolutely identical in the Arabic (Hebrew, Phenician), Greek, and Latin alphabets, as the following synopsis shows. An additional proof is furnished by the identity of the numeral values of the letters in the Arabic and Greek alphabets,—a method totally unknown to the Latins, who must have had a method of their own, probably Etruscan, before they received their alphabet direct from the Phenicians, quite independently of the Greeks, and quite as early.

Arabic.	Greek.	Num.	Latin.
ا	A	1	A
ب	B	2	B
ج	Γ	3	C
د	Δ	4	D
ه	E	5	E
و	Ϛ	6	F
ز	Z	7	G
ح	H	8	H
ط	Θ	9	–
ى	I	10	I
ك	K	20	K
ل	Λ	30	L
م	M	40	M
ن	N	50	N
س	Ξ	60	–

Arabic.	Greek.	Num.	Latin.
ع	O	70	O
ف	Π	80	P
ص	–	90	–

Arabic.	Num.	Greek.	Num.	Latin.
ق¹	100	Ϙ	90	Q
ر	200	P	100	R
ش	300	Σ	200	S
ت	400	T	300	T
ث	500	Υ	400	U
خ	600	Φ	500	V
ذ	700	X	600	X
ض	800	Ψ	700	–
ظ	900	Ω	800	Z
غ	1000	ϡ	900	–

The apparent discrepancies and vacancies occurring on comparison of the three alphabets and the series of numerals, are in reality additional proofs of their absolute identity.

The two first letters call for no remark, though it is known to scholars that the Greek B has been degraded in Rumaic into a *V*, and the so-called modern Greek man is unable to pronounce a *b*, writing it, when necessary, μπ. This combination in Greek words he reads and pronounces as though it were written μβ.

---

1 The Hebrew system is identical with the Arabic as far as its alphabet goes. Thus: ק 100, ר 200, שׁ 300, ת 400; beyond this the words are written in full. This incident is a condemnation of the Greek system for the higher numbers.

The ج, Γ, G, must originally have been a *hard g*. In modern Egyptian, as in Hebrew, and in Greek, it is so pronounced, though the rest of Arabia has softened it into the sound of our English *j* or *soft g*, and though the Latins hardened it, apparently, into a K value.

The first serious remark is called for on our coming to the change made by both the Greeks and the Latins of the Semitic soft aspirate consonant ﻪ into their vowel E. It would almost seem as though the old Phenicians used that letter as a final vowel, exactly as is done by the Persians and Turks at present. A more remarkable divergency, inexplicable to me, but parallel to the foregoing conversion, is the change made by the Greeks of the Semitic hard aspirate consonant ح into their long vowel H, η, whereas the Latins preserved the letter as a consonant and as their sole aspirate, under the same written form as that used by the Greeks, H, h, and which was in reality the Phenician form of the letter.

The next remark is as to the Latin F, which the Greeks long ago discarded from their alphabet, after having in the first instance adopted it in its Phenician form ϝ, and used it to represent the numeral 6. After discarding it as a letter, they continued to use it as a numeral, though with a corrupted, cursive form, ς, to which they still, to this day, give the Phenician name of Bâv, واو, wāw, vāv. The Latin modification of its sound, from a *w* or *v* to an *f*, is of no importance. The Arabs of to-day, having no *v* letter or sound in their language, write the name of Her Majesty the Queen-Empress, *Fiktoriya*.

As the Greek phonetic value of Z exactly corresponds to the Semitic power of ز, their numeral value being identical, and the form of the Latin G being merely a modification, one is tempted to imagine that originally the Latin power of this letter was soft *g*, our *j*, perhaps even our *z*. Certain it is that in some dialects of Italian a *z* is used in words where a soft *g* is found in other dialects.

The Greeks made the Semitic ط into their Θ; the Latins, having no such sound, discarded the letter.

The Semitic ى being both a consonant, like our *y*, and also a long vowel, ī, it followed, as a matter of course, that both Greeks and Latins should make it into the vowel *i*. But the Latins preserved its consonantal use also as an initial; though they forgot, or never realized, that it is a consonant in that position. We now use a *y* to express that value; but the Germans have adopted the Latin modification *j* to represent it. Three western letters, *i, j, y,* are now used for the one Semitic ى.

The next four letters require no comment; but the Semitic س of the eastern Arabs is not a good parallel for the Greek Ξ. The Hebrew letter ם, that holds its place in the alphabet, is the equivalent of the Arabic ص, and the western Arabs of Morocco transpose the س and ص in their أَبًجَد

alphabet, making the fifth word صعفض, the letter ض being
the exact equivalent of the Hebrew צ in place and in power.
The ص is a better representative of צ than the س, but
the two sounds are still very remote from one another.
I should be inclined to suggest that when the Greek alphabet
was formed, the Semitic ش held the place afterwards taken
by the ص and the س. The Greek Ξ is an attempt to
represent our value *sh*, as is seen in the name Xerxes, of
which the old Persian was *Khsharsha*. The Latins dropped
this letter, whichever it really was.

The conversion of Semitic consonantal ع into Greek and
Latin vowel *o* is not unnatural. This letter ع is absolutely
unpronounceable by any other than a Semitic. It is a kind
of convulsion in the throat; and as the two aspirates were
converted into vowels, so was this guttural. This was so
much the more to be expected, as the Semitic letter ا, which
became Greek and Latin *a*, is also a guttural consonant,
serving likewise as a long vowel on occasions. It is the
soft guttural, of which the ع is the hard parallel; and an *o*
may well be looked upon as a hard *a*.

What the Arabians use as *f*, ف, is read in Hebrew, as in
Greek and Latin, *p*. Even the Arabians, when they have
to express a foreign letter, *p*, which they cannot pronounce,
write and pronounce it as a *b*, or as *f*. The next letter, ص
or ض, is dropped in both Greek and Latin. It appears never
to have been used in Greek, even as a numeral; differing in

that respect from the ٮ. When this latter was dropped as a letter, it was retained, modified, as a numeral. But the omitted letter ص became the numeral σάμπι, ϡ representing 900 instead of 90.

From this omission of the ص from its proper place in the Greek numerals, a slip of the whole subsequent series became necessary, so that each letter, from ڧ, Ϙ, Q, onwards, had a higher numeral value by one degree in the Semitic than its representative had in Greek ; ڧ standing for 100, while Ϙ has the value of 90 only ; ر represents 200, while P stands for 100 only ; &c. This slip is very remarkable; it was filled up further on by ϡ 900.

Although the six "additional" letters of the Semitic and Greek alphabets have no relation to each other as representatives of sound, their numerical value goes on exactly in the same order observed in those of the original series, and with the same slip up to غ, representing 1000, while ϡ is only 900. On the other hand, however, the three Greek additionals, υ, φ, χ, are evidently the originals in form of the Latin u, v, x, and the Semitic ظ is possibly the original of the Latin Z. This letter is usually attributed, by ancient and modern authors, to the Greek ζ, which it certainly agrees with in shape, though not in sound.

The forms of the Arabic and Persian Ottoman letters given above are those of the isolated characters. They are liable to various modifications, according to their being initials, medials, or finals, in a combination of written letters.

In the first place, they may, in this respect, be conveniently divided into two classes : those which join on to the following letters in writing a combination, حُرُوفُ وَصْلِيَّة hùrúfù[1] vwâsliyyè, and those which do not so join, حُرُوف مُنْفَصِلَه hùrúfù mùnfâsllâ. The latter, the less numerous class, are: ا, د, ذ, ر, ز, ژ, و and لَام. ,وَر ,ژَاژ ,زَن ,رَب ,ذَج ,دَب ,أَب ,eight in number ; thus, ; ∀

All the others join, as بَا, بَپْ, بَتْ, يَبْ, نَتْ, نَجْ, جَا, چَپْ, حَبْ, ,مِج ,لَج ,كَتْ ,قَتْ ,فَبْ ,غَبْ ,عَا ,ظَج ,طَكْ ,ضَتْ ,صَبْ ,شَبْ ,سَا ,خَج نَج ,هَا ,يَبْ, &c.

All the letters join on in writing to the character that precedes them (other than to the eight enumerated above) whether they be themselves finals or medials. As finals their forms are as follows : بَا, جَبْ, حَبْ, حَتْ, سَتْ, شَج, صَج, ضَج ,تَغْ ,يَعْ ,بَظْ ,يَطْ ,هَض ,نَص ,مَش ,لَس ,كَوْ ,قَز ,فَر ,غَذْ ,عَدْ ,طَج ظَلَا. ,طَى ,ضَه ,صُو ,شَن ,سَم ,خَل ,حَكْ ,جَقْ ,تَفْ As medials they are figured thus : بَابْ, حَبْ, تَپْر, سَتَر, شَكَلْ, بَجَن, مَچَا, سَحَا, شَحَبْ,

---

[1] It having been found impracticable to mark in type the varying Ottoman tone-values of the Arabian and Persian long vowels, the student must learn to supply the numbers 1 and 2 over the long-vowel marks. For this purpose, he must apply the rules for the short vowels, according as they follow, or are followed by, a consonant of the soft or hard class. By practice, the correct habit will be thus acquired ; the case of the short vowels teaching the tone, which will then be instinctively used when the vowel is long.

نَكَظْ , ضَقَلْ , صَفَرْ , ضَغْتْ , بَعَتْ , بَظَرْ , سَطْرِ , خَضَنْ , فَصْلْ , عَشَرْ , طَشَت , كَكَرْ , نَمَرْ , جَنَتْ , جَهَلْ , مِينْ   Those which do not join are, as medials, thus written : بَابْ , هَدَرْ , بَذَلْ , فَرَطْ , جَزَمْ , بِزُمِرْدَه , صَوْبْ , لَازِ . Longer combinations vary, *ad infinitum*, as follows : حَرْفَتْ , رَنْجَبَرْلِكْ , أُوتُورْمَغْلَه , كَلْمَيْنْجَه , تَجَاهُلْ , مُتَنَاظِرْ , قَايِلُونْ , مُتَوَسِّطْ , احْتِجَاجْ , عَدَالَتْ , يَادِشَاهَانَه , قَاضِيعَسْكَرْلِكْ , &c.

Besides the simple names of the letters hitherto mentioned, most of the characters have other, more complicated appellations.

The ا is usually called hĕmzĕ, هَمْزِ, when a consonant, in an Arabic word ; and ĕllfĭ mĕmdūdĕ, أَلِفِ مَمْدُودَه, *prolonged* ا, when it is a long vowel, initial or medial. It can never be a *long final* vowel in an Arabic word, being then always followed by another consonant hĕmzĕ ; as, شَاءِ shā'ĕ, جَزَاءِ jĕzā'ĕ, &c. It is called ĕllfĭ mâqsūrĕ, أَلِفِ مَقْصُورَه, *shortened* ا, when final. It is then more commonly written ى in classical Arabic ; but by no means always so. In Persian and Turkish, or foreign words, the ا is always a vowel, but is called indifferently ĕllf and hĕmzĕ. It is always long in Persian words, when medial or final. When initial in a Persian word, it may be short or long. When a long initial, it is distinguished, as in Arabic, by the sign mĕdd, مَدْ (~) over it, as : A. آفَتْ āfĕt, P. آبْ āb. When a short initial, it is, in Arabic, generally a consonant, and may take the sound 'ă or 'ĕ, of 'l,

or of 'û. When a short initial in Persian, it is a vowel, and
may have any one of the three values â or ê, i, û. The details
of the powers of ١ in Turkish words are given further on.

The ب is distinguished from the other letters of the same
isolated form by being called بَاء مُوَحَّدَ (bā'l mûvâhhâdê), *the
single-dotted* ب ; as the ت is named تَاء مُثَنَّات (tā'l mûsnât),
the double-dotted ت, and the ث is designated ثَاء مُثَلَّثَ (sā'l mû-
sêllêsê), *the triply-dotted* ث. The ت is further distinguished
from the ط, also named tâ, طا, by being called تَاء قَرَشَتْ (tā'l
qârâshât), *the* ت *of* (the word) قَرَشَتْ ; while ط is named
طَاء حُطِّى (tā'l hûttī), *the* ط *of* (the word) حُطِّى. Again, the ت
is distinguished, as a medial or initial, from the ى, then identical in form with it, by being called مُثَنَاتِ فَوْقِيَّة (mûsnâtl fêv-
qiyyê), *superiorly double-dotted ;* whereas the ى is then
termed مُثَنَاتِ تَحْتَانِيَّه (mûsnâtl tâhtānlyyê), *inferiorly double-
dotted.* The ث is also called ثَاء نَخَذ (ŧā'l sâkhâz), *the* ث *of* نَخَذ.
The ب might be called بَاء أَبْجَدْ (bā'l êbjêd), *the* ب *of* ابجد ; but
I do not recollect the expression. It is, however, distinguished from the Persian پ by being designated بَاء عَرَبِيَّه (bā'l
'ârâbīyyê), *the Arabian* ب, the پ being called بَاء فَارِسِيَّه (bā'l
fârlslyyê), and بَاء عَجَمِيَّه (bā'l 'âjâmlyyê), *the Persian* پ.

The simple name of the ج, جيم jīm, sufficiently distinguishes
the letter from all other Arabic characters. It has, therefore,
no other designation in purely Arabic works. It is, however,

distinguished from the Persian چ by their being styled respectively جِيمِ عَرَبِيَّه (jīmĭ 'årĕbĭyyĕ), and جِيمِ فَارِسِيَّه (jīmĭ fārĭsĭyyĕ),
or جِيمِ عَجَمِيَّه (jīmĭ 'åjåmĭyyĕ).

The ح and خ are distinguished from one another by the
terms حَاءِ مُهْمَلَه (hā'ĭ mŭhmĕlĕ) *neglected* (undotted) ح, and
خَاءِ مُعْجَمَه (khā'ĭ mŭ'jĕmĕ) *distinguished* (dotted) خ, respectively.
In Persian they are often called حَاءِ بِينُقْطَه (hā'ĭ bī-nŭqtå) *dotless*
ح, and خَاءِ نَقْطَهدَارْ (khā'ĭ nŭqtå-dår) *dot-possessing* (dotted) خ.
These two pairs of Arabic and Persian adjectives go all
through the alphabet, in the cases where a dot is the sole
distinction between two letters of the same form; as, دَالِ مُهْمَلَه
(dālĭ mŭhmĕlĕ) د; ذَالِ مُعْجَمَه (zālĭ mŭ'jĕmĕ) ذ. So also the
distinctions by the words of the " numeral alphabet ;" as,
دَالِ أَبْجَدْ (dålĭ ĕbjĕd), ذَالِ نَخَذْ (zālĭ såkhåz), ذ; رَاءِ قَرَشَتْ (rā'ĭ
qåråshåt) ر; زَاءِ هَوَّزْ (zā'ĭ hĕvvĕz) ز; &c.; سِينِ مُهْمَلَه (sīnĭ mŭhmĕlĕ), س; شِينِ مُعْجَمَه (shīnĭ mŭ'jĕmĕ), ش; &c.

When we come to ف, the written names of the letters are
so distinct of themselves, that no addition is necessary for
فَا (fā), ف; قَافْ (qāf), ق; كَافْ (kyāf, *vulgarly* kĕf), ك;
لَامْ (lām), ل; مِيمْ (mīm), م; نُونْ (nūn), ن; وَاوْ (vwāw), و.
With ه a distinction again comes in, to differentiate the letter
from ح. We, therefore, say هَاءِ هَوَّزْ (hā'ĭ hĕvvĕz), ه; as the
ح is then termed حَاءِ حُطِّي (hā'ĭ hŭtti); and ى is termed, as

mentioned above, يَاءِ مُثَنَّاتٍ تَحْتَانِيَّه (yā'ı̇ mûsnātı̇ tâhtānı̇yyė); being also called يَاءِ حُطِّى (yā'ı̇ hûttı̇).

The Persian پ and چ are distinguished as is described above; and in like manner the ژ is called زَاءِ فَارِسِيَّه (zā'ı̇ fārı̇syyė), and زَاءِ عَجَمِيَّه (zâ'ı̇ 'âjâmı̇yyė).

There remains now to distinguish, among consonants, the different sorts of ك used in Ottoman Turkish, and to point out their several names, as follows : The original Arabian ك is named كَاف عَرَبِيَّه (kyāfı̇ 'ârêbı̇yyė, *vulg.* kêfı̇ 'ârêbī), *the Arabian* ك; its value is that of our *k.* This letter was next used by the Persians for their *hard g;* it was then, and is still, distinguished by the name of كَاف فَارِسِيَّه (kyāfı̇ fārı̇syyė, *vulg.* kyāfı̇ fārı̇sī, kêfı̇ fārı̇sī), and كَاف عَجَمِيَّه (kyāfı̇ 'âjâmı̇yyė, *vulg.* kêfı̇ 'âjâmı̇). This variety is sometimes distinguished, in writing, in one or the other of two different methods. The Persians themselves mark the difference by doubling the upper dash of the letter in all its written variations—isolated, initial, medial, and final; thus : سگ, مگر, گل, گ; whereas the original Arabian ك, when isolated or final, has no dash at all; as, اَبُوك, ابنَك; and a single dash, when initial or medial; thus: كدر, نكته, also shaped كدته, نكته.

When these two values of the one letter ك passed into use for the Ottoman language, a new mode of distinguishing the Persian from the Arabian variety was introduced. It con-

sisted of placing three dots over the Arabian form of the ك,
together with a single dash in non-final positions; thus : كُلّ‎, نَ‎,
مَكَرّ‎, سَنْك‎; thus marking the Persian *hard g* value of the
letter.

But this letter, so differentiated in Persian writing, received
in Ottoman Turkish a third value, that of our consonantal *y*,
as a softened variety of its Persian value of *hard g*. This
Ottoman value never occurs elsewhere than at the end, or
in the middle of a word; as : بَك‎ (bèy), يَكَنَّك‎ (bèyánmèk),
يِكِرِمِي‎ (yiyirmi), ايكِرنَمَك‎ (iyránmèk). In the middle of a word
it may begin or end a syllable : bè-yán-mèk, iy-rán-mèk.
When this letter follows a *u* vowel, and is itself followed by
an *e* vowel, it glides into the value of our *w*; as سُوَك‎
(sûwè), &c.

In Turkish, the ك, retaining the same form, received
another value still, the fourth; being then for distinction's
sake, called *surd* ن, صَاغِرْ نُون‎ (sághìr nūn) ; as in اَك‎ (èñ),
آكْمَق‎ (åñmáq), سَنِك‎ (sánìñ), قُوصَكُورْ‎ (qòñdùr). This value
is never initial. When medial, it may begin, and may also
end a syllable, as it ends many words. The three dots over
the ك, mentioned in the preceding paragraph, are used by
some to designate this Turkish value of *surd* ن ; and at other
times a single dot is used for that purpose, leaving the three
dots to mark the Persian value of the letter. These varying

values of the ل constitute a serious difficulty in learning to read Ottoman Turkish. *Surd* ن is here transliterated ñ.

A similar variation in the phonetic value of the Arabic letter غ is to be observed in Ottoman Turkish words. Originally it is, in an Ottoman mouth, a simple hard *g ;* as : غَالِبْ (gālĭb), أَغْلَبْ (ăglĕb), مَغْلُوبْ (măglūb). In Turkish words it has a softened value, very much like that of our *gh*, but still more softened, even to the point of practically disappearing from the pronunciation ; as : طَاغْ (dăgh, almost dăw), طَاغِنْ (dăghĭñ, almost dă'ĭñ), طَاغَدَ (dăghă, dă'ă), طَاغِى (dăghĭ, dă'ĭ), طَاغْدَنْ (dă'dăn), طَاغِدَ (dă'dă), &c. When preceded by an *o* or *u* vowel, the غ, in Turkish words, if followed by a vowel, glides into the value of our *w*, even as our own *gh* does in the word *throughout* (pronounced *thruwout*) ; as : طُوغَانْ (dŏwăn), صُوغَانْ (sŏwăn), قُوغُشْ (qŏwŭsh) ; or it nearly disappears in pronunciation, as before ; thus : أُولْدِيغِمْ (ŏldŭwŭm, or oldu'um), أُولْدِيغِى (ŏldŭwŭ, or ŏldŭ'ŭ).

SECTION II. *The Phonetic Values of the Letters and Vowel-Points, the Uses of the other Orthographic Signs, our System of Transliteration, and the Doctrine of Ottoman Euphony.*

We must divide the thirty-one Ottoman letters (omitting ﻻ) into vowels and consonants. But it must first be premised that every letter is sometimes a consonant, while only four of them are sometimes vowels. These are ‏ا , و , ء , ی‎ . All the others, twenty-seven in form, are always consonants. It will be more convenient to treat of the four vowel letters first, together with the vowel-points, which are not letters, but simply marks.

Usually, the vowel-points, three only in number, are not written; they are supposed to be known. But, in children's books, in Qur'ans, in books of devotion, &c., they are written; and sometimes in other books and papers also.

The vowel-points are named: 1, ûstûn, ‏اوستون‎ (over), the mark of which is a short diagonal from the right downwards towards the left, placed *over* any consonant; as: ‏بَ , تَ , جَ‎ , &c.; 2, ésêrê, ‏اَسَرِ‎ (no meaning), a similar diagonal, marked *under* any consonant; as: ‏ح , خِ , دِ , ذِ‎ , &c.; 3, ûtûrû, ‏اوتورو‎ (no meaning), a small ‏و‎-shaped mark, placed *over* any consonant; as: ‏رُ , زُ , رُ , سُ‎ , &c.

These vowel-points mark, originally, the three Arabic short vowels, to which the additional Ottoman vowel-sounds, à, â, â have been added. The ûstûn has the value of à or ê, according to the consonant, &c., accompanying it; the ésêrê has the value of ì or î; and the ûtûrû that of ò, û, û, û, also according to its accompaniment.

The short vowel-sound indicated by each of these three marks always follows, in pronunciation, the sound of the consonant to which it is appended; so that we have the following

Ottoman syllabary, No. 1 : بَ bá, bå, bẳ, bả, bẻ ; بِ bĭ, bĭ ; بُ bỏ, bú, bẳ, bử ; and so on through the alphabet.

When it is required to make the vowel long, one of the three Arabic *letters of prolongation,* حَرْف مَدّ (hárfĭ médd, *pl.* حُرُوف مَدّ hŭrūfĭ médd), has to be added to the consonant, still marked with its short vowel-point. The letters of prolonga-tion, true *long vowels,* are ا, و, ى ; of which ا always accom-panies ûstûn, ى always accompanies ésérè; and و always accompanies ûtûrû. We now have Ottoman syllabary No. 2, as follows : بَا bā, bā ; بِى bī, bī ; بُو bō, bū, bū, bū ; &c.

We thus see that there are eleven Ottoman short vowels, and eight long. Our system of transliterating them is also made apparent. It is the simple method of using *a* or *e* to represent ûstûn, *i* to represent ésérè, and *o* or *u* to represent ûtûrû. As these vowel-points shade off in phonetic value, we use á, å, ẳ, ả, or è for ûstûn ; ĭ or ĭ for ésérè ; and ỏ, or ú, ů, ử, for ûtûrû. After long consideration, we have for some years past adopted this system, as the simplest, and, on the whole, the most rational.

The values of these Ottoman vowels are those of the vowels in the following eleven words. They are all familiar English words, excepting the French *tu,* the vowel of which is unknown in ordinary English, though it exists in the dialects of some of our counties. These words are: *far, war, a-*(bove),

pan, pen ; pin, girl ; so ; put, tu, cur. We mark the vowels
of these eleven guide-words to the Ottoman pronunciation, in
the order in which they stand : fär, wär, åbove, pån, pêu, pĭn,
gĭrl, só, pŭt, tå, cŭr ; and for the eight Ottoman long vowels
we use: fär, wār, pīn, gīrl, sō, pūt, tū, cūr. That is, nineteen
Ottoman vowel-sounds in all, long and short. The student
has but to remember the series of ten English words and one
French, to become possessed of the key to the Ottoman vowel
pronunciation. But he must learn never to swerve from the
values of those guide-vowels. To an Englishman, with our
slouchy method, this unswervingness is the most difficult
point ; but, with a little patience at first, it is to be achieved.
He must practice himself in pronouncing påshå, بَاشَا (not
påshåw), båbå, بَابَا (not båybå), dån, دَن (not dèn), sån, سَن
(not sèn), bèn, بَن (which he will at once pronounce right),
ĭs-(tèmèk), اِسْتَمَك, fĭr-(låmåq), فِرْلَامَق, qôl, قُول (not qål),
qŭl, قُل (not qŭl), yåz, يُوز (not yŭz or yåz), and gyåz, كُوز
(not gyåz or gyåz, though these are also words or syllables).

The English student of Turkish has to exert his utmost
care, in respect of the Ottoman vowels, to break himself of
the home method of pronouncing a short vowel, and the same
vowel when long, in two very different ways. The Ottoman
vowels remain always pure ; they never change in phonetic
value with a change in phonetic *quantity;* thus, ă is always å

ma.le long; ī is always 1 long, ō is always ô long, ū is always û long, &c., in the same word and its derivatives.

The student will have noticed above the Arabic *sign of quiescence* of a consonant. It is named jĕzm, جْزْم and is never placed over a vowel, long or short.

The fourth Ottoman vowel letter, ه, which, when a consonant, is the soft aspirate *h*, is also derived from the Arabic, but has a special history of its own. This letter is never used as a vowel in Arabic in any other position than that of a final to a noun, substantive or adjective, usually of the feminine gender, sometimes singular, and sometimes an irregular (*broken*, technically) plural. Such are the words— خَلِيفَه khâlīfè, سُنَّه sûnnè, حَسَنَه hâsânâ, طَيِّبَه tâyyibè, &c.

In Arabic, these pronunciations (as modified in Ottoman Turkish, as to the vowels, and as to the consonants) are those of the words when they close a sentence or clause in classical reading. They are also the pronunciations of the words in modern conversational Arabic.

But, originally, and to this day, in classical Arabic, those and all such words end not in a vowel at all. They all end in a consonant, in a letter *t*; which, for certain grammatical reasons, is never figured ت, but always appears in the shape of a letter ه surmounted by the two dots of the ت, thus ة. Our specimen words are therefore, originally, خَلِيفَة khâlīfèt, سُنَّة sûnnèt, حَسَنَة hâsânèt, طَيِّبَة tâyyibèt. There are other vowels and consonants to be added to the termination of these in classical Arabic, to mark the case-endings or declinations. Thus خَلِيفَة, when definite, may be marked خَلِيفَةُ khâlîfêtû for the nominative, خَلِيفَةِ khâlîfêtî for the genitive, خَلِيفَةَ khâlîfêtâ for the accusative. When indefinite, it becomes خَلِيفَةٌ khâlîfêtûn, خَلِيفَةٍ khâlîfêtîn, خَلِيفَةً khâlîfêtân. In all these cases, when final in a sentence or clause, the case-endings are dropped from the pronunciation, though still written in vowel-pointed books, and the word becomes simply khâlîfê throughout. These indefinite case-ending marks are called in Turkish اِيكِى اُوتُورُو (îkî ûtûrû), *double* ûtûrû, اِيكِى اَسَرَو (îkî êsêrê), *double* êsêrê, and اِيكِى اُوستُونْ (îkî ûstûn) *double* ûstûn.

A consideration now arose. In classical Arabic, final consonants may be either silent, or vocal with any one of the three short vowels. Thus : كَتَبَتْ kêtêbêt, كَتَبْتُ kêtêbtû, كَتَبْتَ kêtêbtâ, كَتَبْتِ kêtêbtî. When such words are final in a sentence or clause, the final consonant is made silent; so that we have kêtêbêt, as before, for the first ; but kêtêbt for all three of the remaining words. So نَصْرَ, نَصْرِ, نَصْرُ, final, becomes nâsr, as does نَصْرُ and نَصْرِ, though نَصْرً (always distinguished by a servile ا being added—نَصْرًا nâsrân) remains fully pronounced, or only loses the sound of the final *n*, and is read nâsrâ.

When the final ة of خَلِيفَة khâlîfê, and similar words, was dropped from the pronunciation, the letter might have been

dropped in writing also; for خَلِیفَ would read khâlîfè just
as well. It could, however, and would, be read خَلِیفْ khâlîf,
as Europe has done in making it into *Caliph*. It was necessary, then, to devise a method which should prevent the
suppression of the vowel belonging to the last consonant of
such words, and yet not be liable to be pronounced as a *t*
with the case-endings. This convenient method was dis-
covered by the arrangement adopted of suppressing the dots
of the ة, and leaving the nude ه appended to the word, as
خَلِیفَه khâlîfè, &c. By this method final ه in such words
became virtually a vowel in Arabic, though it is never mentioned as such in Arabic grammars or lexicons.

Persian has a very large number of nouns, substantive and
adjective, that end in an ûstûn vowel. When the Arabic
alphabet became the sole mode of writing Persian, the Arab
teachers would naturally use their quasi-vowel final ه to
represent that final Persian sound. Thus, بَرَ bèrè, سُغْرَنَ sû-
gûrnè, آمَادَه âmâdè, رَسِیدَ rèsîdè, &c., were written. The ه
was thus made a vowel in Persian also, when final. It was
even made to follow one of the other two short vowels in
very rare cases, when no other device was available. Thus
we have the numeral سَه (sì), *three* (in Ottoman Turkish
usually pronounced سَه sè), کَ (kì), *that*, چَ (chì), *what, that.*

When, by another historical step, Turkish began to be
written in the Arabic characters modified by the special

Persian letters (Turkish scribes learning the method from Persian teachers in the land of Persia conquered by Turkish invaders, who there embraced Islam), the use of ه as a final vowel was found so convenient as to be naturally adopted. So اَبَه èbè, آطَا ádá, &c., were written. Now, a whole class of Turkish gerunds, optatives, and imperatives of the third person, end with this vowel ; we, therefore, have ایدَه ìdè, کیدَه gìdè, کُورَه gyûrè, قَالَ qálá, قِیرَه qìrá, &c.

A further step was, therefore, possible to be taken in Ottoman Turkish, from which Persian writers had and have shrunk. The vowel ه was used as a medial also, whenever it was found that its introduction served to distinguish two words written alike, but pronounced differently. Thus بِلْمَك bìlmèk, could also be read بِلَمَك bìlèmèk. If the vowel-points were always marked, they would suffice for this case ; but they are generally omitted. The gerund and optative بِلَه or بِیلَه was already in use. By writing بِلْمَك bìlmèk and بِیلَمَك bìlèmèk, the distinction was made clear. Hence, ه as a medial Ottoman vowel, always indicating a preceding ûstûn short vowel-point, became fully established. This medial or final Turkish vowel ه never joins on to the next letter in writing; as, اُورَمَك ûrèmèk, اُوطَدَه ôdádá.

From this sketch of the history of final and medial vowel ه, we see plainly how fundamentally erroneous is the common

European (or rather English) method of transliterating such words with a final or medial *h*. The nearest approach to correctness of which our orthography is capable, since we possess not the French *é* or German *e*, is to write all such words with a final *a*, as *khalifa, Fatima, Mekka, Medina, Brusa*, &c. These are usual ; but جِدّ‍ه *Jidda*, is usually spelt *Jeddah ;* while قَاهِرَه *Qāhira* (usually *Cairo*), طَنْجَه *Tanja* (usually *Tangiers*), &c., have been made into monstrosities.

The phonetic value of an initial ا is at first a difficulty to the European student, inasmuch as there appears to be nothing like it in Western languages. This, however, is more apparent than real, when fully explained.

We must remember that in Arabic the initial ا or أ is a *consonant*, not a vowel. Like any other initial consonant, it takes the three short vowel-points, and is then pronounced: أ ›è, إ ›ì, أ ›ù. When it became a Persian letter, it was generally named *hèmzè*, as it is usually called in Arabic when a consonant (but never when a vowel of prolongation, or final and short); although, in Persian words, it is always a vowel, whether initial, medial, or final. With the short vowel-points, this initial ا is always a short vowel in Persian words, and the Arabian *hèmzè* sign is never placed over it ; thus: اَر *èr,* اَز *èz,* اَسْب *èsb,* اَسْت *èst,* &c.; اِسْپَاه *ispāh,* اِصْفَاهَان *ìsfāhān,* &c.; اُلاغ *ùlāg,* &c.

This initial short vowel Persian system was extended (in *practice*, not in *theory*) to all Arabic words used in Persian with ‏ا‎ for their initial letter. But the Arabic consonantal ‏ا‎ was then taken (in practice) to be a Persian vowel ‏ا‎. Thus, ‏اَبْوَابْ‎ was read ĕbvāb, ‏اِبْتِدَا‎ ĭbtĭdă, ‏اُصُولْ‎ ŭsūl ; &c.

When, in Arabic, the vowel of the initial consonantal ‏ا‎ became long, then, *as with any other initial consonant,* a vowel letter of prolongation,—a long vowel letter,—was appended to the ‏ا‎ ; thus: ‏اا‎, pronounced ꞌā, ‏اُو‎, pronounced ꞌū, ‏اِى‎, pronounced ꞌī.

This system passed also into use in Persian words, the Arabic hĕmzĕ sign being omitted, even in Arabic words adopted into Persian ; and thus the combinations ‏اا‎, ‏اُو‎, ‏اِى‎, became the initial Persian long vowels ; being pronounced respectively—ā, ū, ī. Thus : ‏اابْ‎ āb, ‏اُوبَارْ‎ ūbār, ‏اِيزَدْ‎ īzĕd ; and with words originally Arabic : ‏اابَا‎ ābā, ‏اُولَا‎ ūlā, ‏اِيمَا‎ īmā ; &c.

The Arabians found the use of ‏اا‎ somewhat cumbersome. They therefore invented a sign, ˜, called mĕddă, ‏مَدَّ‎, and ‏مَدّ‎ mĕdd, to be placed over an initial ‏ا‎, with or without the hĕmzĕ sign, to designate the long vowel. Thus, instead of ‏اابَا‎, they wrote ‏آبَا‎ ꞌābā, &c. The Persians adopted this system also, writing ‏آبْ‎ āb instead of ‏اابْ‎. The double ‏ا‎ system, however, is still to be found in use in native Persian lexicons ; where the first section of chapter ‏ا‎ is generally figured with the two ‏اا‎, not with ‏آ‎.

It may be useful to mention here, that the Arabian writers employ this sign of mèdd to mark a medial or a quasi-final long vowel ١, whenever this is followed in the word by a hèmzè, *i. e.*, a consonantal ١. Thus they write يَتَسَاءَلُوَن yètèsā-ٔàlùnà, حَمْرَاآ hàmrāٔù, &c. These mèdd signs are omitted in Persian, as well as the final ٔ ; so that حَمْرَا hàmrā is written, as well as pronounced, for حَمْرَاآ ; &c.

If a medial consonantal hèmzè in an Arabic word be followed by a long vowel ١, the two are united, as in the initial آ, into one ١ letter with the mèdd sign over it ; as مَآل màٔāl (for مَأَال). This also is adopted in Persian with such Arabic words as it occurs in ; not being found in any original Persian words.

The mèdd sign is also used, in Arabic, sometimes taking another form, that of a small, perpendicular ٰ, to mark the traditional omission, in writing (not in pronunciation), of a long vowel ١ in a few well-known words, such as الٰه ٔllāh (for الٰه), إِلٰهِي ٔllāhī (for الٰهِي), رَحْمٰن or رَحْمَٰن ràhmān (for رَحْمَان), &c.

This perpendicular small èlìf-shaped mèdd is also placed, in Arabic, sometimes over a letter و, to mark that, though radically a و, it is a long vowel ١ in pronunciation, in the two words only, حَيٰوة hàyāt (usually written حَيَاة, in Persian and Turkish حَيَات) and صَلٰوة sàlāt (usually written صَلَاة, in Persian and Turkish صَلَات).

The mèdd sign is sometimes placed, in Arabic, over a long vowel و or ى, when they ɛre followed by a hèmzè in the same word ; as in سُوّد sūᵽd, جِیّ jiᵽd. This peculiarity is not used in Persian or Turkish.

It is also sometimes placed over a long vowel medial ١, when this letter is followed by a reduplicated consonant in the same word ; as: مَآدَّ mᾱddè; it is not used in Persian or Turkish.

Such of the foregoing Arabic usages as have been adopted in Persian for words of Persian or of Arabic origin, are also employed in Ottoman Turkish for the same words ; though they are sometimes omitted in ordinary writing.

We now come to a purely Ottoman use of the mèdd sign, utterly unknown in Arabic and Persian. Thus : Whenever an initial vowel ١ of an Ottoman word of Turkish or foreign (European or Indian) origin has the short sound of à or å, the mèdd sign is placed over it, as a distinction from the initial sounds å, å, è; as : آمِیرَال àmīràl (French), آرى àrı, آطه àdà (Turkish); but أَصَلَتْ àsālèt, أَوَّل àvvàl (Arabic), أَرْ èr (Turkish ; also Persian ; but two different words).

Another Ottoman peculiarity connected with the initial ١, when followed in writing by a vowel و or ى, is that these two vowels are not *necessarily* long vowels in words of Turkish or foreign origin. Thus أُوت òt, أُور ùr, أُوتُو ùtù, أُوتْمَكْ ùtmèk, أُوفِچَال òfìchàl, اِیرْلانْدَه ìrlàndà. They may then be called *directing vowels.* In many old or provincial books and writings, these directing vowels are often or systematically omitted, the writers, from habit, or system, adhering to the original Arabic method of spelling by short vowel-points, for the most part omitted in current writing. This makes such books and papers immensely difficult to read and understand.

The three Arabic long vowels, ا, و, ى, having thus acquired a footing as Ottoman short directing-vowels, when following an initial letter ا, it was found convenient to extend the system, and to use them as short directing-vowels, following initial or medial consonants, thereby departing entirely from the Arabic and Persian systems. There is no method in use for distinguishing a long vowel letter from a short one in an Ottoman word of Turkish or foreign origin. We may almost venture to say that all such medial vowel-letters in Turkish and foreign Ottoman words are short vowels; whereas, in Arabic and Persian words they are always long. Thus: باش bâsh, قِر qĭr, قُوش qûsh, اَغْلَامَق âghlâmâq, صِيزِلْدِى sĭzĭldĭ, بُوزُلْمَق bôzŭlmâq, بُوزُلْمَك bûzŭlmĕk, كُورُلْدِى gyûrûldû, كُورُنْمَك gyûrûnmĕk.

Hitherto we have considered only the *open* syllables, that is, those which end with a vowel. We have now to treat of the closed syllables,—those which end with a consonant.

In the original Arabic system, when a word or syllable ended with a *quiescent* consonant,—a consonant not followed

by a vowel sound or vowel letter in the same syllable,—such
consonant was marked, in pointed writings, by the sign °
placed over it, which, as was before remarked, is called jĕzm,
جَزْم . Thus : بَبْ bĕb, بَابْ bāb, بُوبْ būb, بيب bīb, &c.

It is a rule in classical Arabic, that two quiescent consonants cannot follow one another in the same syllable,
whether as initials or as finals. Such a word or syllable as
crust, tart, blurt, flirt, &c., is unknown. As far as two such
initial consonants go, this rule prevails in the vernacular
Arabic also, and has passed into the Persian and Turkish.
Foreign words with such combinations of initial consonants
to words or syllables are treated in one of two ways. When
initial in a word, they may be separated into two syllables,
either by a servile vowel ١, generally with an ĕsĕrĕ vowel,
being prefixed ; or by a vowel, generally ĕsĕrĕ, being intercalated ; and when the combination is initial to a non-initial
syllable of a word, the latter method alone is used, or the
syllables are so divided as to separate the two consonants.
Thus : κλίμα has become اِقْليم ïqlīm, *kral* has become قِرَالْ qïrāl,
prince has become پِرِنْج pïrïnj, and *Svizzera* has become اِسْويچَرْ
ïsvïchĕr.

In classical Arabic, a final word in a phrase or clause could
terminate in two quiescent consonants ; as : رَبْطْ rābt, عِلْمْ 'llm,
حَزْنْ hūzn, &c. This liberty is much used in Persian, Turkish,

and foreign, as well as in Arabic Ottoman words; thus :
دُرُسْت dŭrŭst, آرْد ârd, پِرِنْس pĭrĭns, پِرِنْج pĭrĭnj (*prince*); &c.

When a letter in an Arabic word ends one syllable, and
begins the next in the same word, it is not written twice,
but one sole letter is made to serve for the two, in pointed
writings, by having a special mark, ˝, placed over it. This
mark is an abbreviation of the Arabic word شَدّ shĕdd, which
means a *strengthening, corroboration, reduplication.* Thus we
have, شِدَّت shĭddĕt, عِلَّت 'ĭllet, بَقَّال bâqqāl, عَطَّار 'âttār, مَدّ mĕdd,
وِدّ vĭdd, اُمّ ŭmm, &c. It is a *sine quâ non* in Ottoman reading,
and in correct speaking, to redouble such letters in the pronunciation. We can derive a correct idea of this reduplication
by studying our expressions, *mid-day, ill-luck, run next,* &c.
But, if such reduplicated Arabic word has passed into vernacular Ottoman use, then the redoubling is excused in
ordinary conversation ; as in the words بَقَّال bâqâl, عَطَّار
âqtâr ; &c.

This reduplication is really unknown in Persian ; consequently, reduplicated Arabic words are much used in
Persian without reduplication; thus خَطّ is generally used in
Persian as خَط khât, and has thence, as similar words, passed
into Ottoman Turkish. On the other hand, pedantic imitation
has commonly given to a few Persian words the Arabic peculiarity of reduplication, so passing into Ottoman also : thus,

بَر pèr (*a wing*), is sometimes pronounced بَرّ pèrr ; and بَرَنْدَه pèrèndè, بَرَّنْدَه pèrrèndè ; &c.

This reduplicating system is not used in correctly writing Turkish Ottoman words, but it is sometimes met with in incorrect writings. The two letters should be written in full in such Turkish words; thus, جُوْلُّق chùllùq, بُوْلُّق bòllùq, اَمَّكْ èmmèk, &c.

The Arabic word hèmzè, هَمْزَه, besides being a name for the letter ا, as before explained, is also the name of an orthographic sign, mark, or point, very variously used in Arabic and Persian. Most of the rules concerning it, which derive from the two languages, have passed into Ottoman Turkish, with an addition or two used in the Turkish transliteration of foreign words. Turkish words never require the sign.

The hèmzè sign, ء, would appear to be a diminutive head of the letter ع, thus indicating to the eye the guttural nature of the vocal enunciation it represents; which is, in fact, a softened choke, in an Arab mouth. But in Persian and Turkish pronunciation it is a slight *hiatus*, at the beginning of a non-initial syllable, or at the end of any syllable, initial, medial or final. It is placed *over* a letter when it bears the ùstùn or ùtùrù vowel, or is quiescent; *under* it, generally, with the èsèrè vowel.

The hèmzè, in a word of Arabic origin, always represents a consonantal letter ا, sometimes radical, sometimes servile.

In Persian words, the *theory* of the sign is the same as in Arabic, but the sign itself is always servile, and either final or nearly so.

When a hèmzè, radical or servile, is initial in an Arabic word, it is never written or pronounced in Persian or Turkish. The ا letter is then taken to be a vowel, and is treated accordingly. Thus, اَمَل ᵓèmèl, becomes اَمَل èmèl; ابِل ᵓIbIl, becomes ابِل IbIl; اُم ᵓûmm, becomes اُم ûmm. These are all radicals, and short. So again, اَفَكَر ᵓèfkyār, becomes اَفَكَر èfkyār; اِقَبَال ᵓIqbāl, becomes اِقَبَال Iqbāl; اَمُور ᵓûmūr, becomes اَمُور ûmūr; &c. These initials are all servile, and short. The modes and doctrine of making them into long vowels have already been described. In Persian, Turkish, and foreign words, an initial ا is always a vowel, and is made long in the same way as if the word were of Arabic origin, as has been said before.

When a hèmzè, radical or servile, in an Arabic word, is medial or final, a rather numerous body of rules come into play. Sometimes the letter ا, then always called hèmzè, is written, together with the hèmzè sign over it, أ (as in رَأْس rèᵓs), and sometimes the hèmzè sign above is figured, as a letter now, without the ا, in the body of the word; as in يَتَسَاءَلُون yètèsāᵓèlūn. In the former of these two cases, the hèmzè is usually a final, quiescent consonant in its syllable; as, رَأْفَت rèᵓ-fèt, مَأْمَن mèᵓ-mèn, &c. In the latter case, the hèmzè is the initial consonant of its medial or final syllable, movent with

ûstûn ; as in اجُزْ jûz-ân, اجِزْءاً jézâ-ân, &c. But it may also
be both ; that is, a quiescent hémzé may terminate one syllable,
while another, a movent hémzé, may begin the next syllable.
In this case, as with any other consonant so occurring, one ا
alone is written, with a hémzé sign over it ; and above this,
the téshdīd sign is superadded, with an ûstûn sign over it
again ; as in تَعَأَلّ téfé-·él. This step never occurs in Turkish
phrases ; but the explanation is needed, so as to make clear
what follows.

This reduplicated medial hémzé, movent with ûstûn, is
sometimes followed by a long vowel ا. In this case, instead
of writing, for instance, رَأْأس rá-·ās, the two letters ا are combined into one, with the signs médd and hémzé, and without
the ûstûn vowel ; thus, رَأس rá-·ās, as before. This combination is of very rare occurrence, happening only in derivative
words, of which the root is triliteral, with hémzé for second
radical.

But a movent initial hémzé of a syllable, medial in a word,
may be followed by a long vowel ا, without being reduplicated.
It is then figured by a single written ا with the hémzé and
médd signs ; as, مأال má-·āl, &c.

These combinations, when used in Turkish, drop the hémzé
and téshdīd signs, but preserve the médd sign. The ûstûn
vowel that precedes such médd sign is hardened from é into â,

on account of the following ā, even with a preceding soft consonant.

But, when such medial or final hèmzè is itself movent with èsèrè, it is no longer written in the form of ا; it then takes the form of ى, without dots, and with a hèmzè sign over it; as, رَئِيس rèʼīs. If its vowel is ùtùrù, it is written as a و letter, with hèmzè sign over it; as, رُؤُوس rùʼūs. In these two examples the vowels are long; but there are words in Arabic some perchance used in Turkish, in which they are short. Of course, the long vowel letters do not then follow the modified, disguised hèmzè. Thus, رَائِس rāʼis, أَبُؤْس èbʼùs.

Moreover, when such medial or final hèmzè, whether movent or quiescent, is preceded by a consonant movent with èsèrè, the hèmzè is figured as a letter ى; and when movent with ùtùrù, the hèmzè is written as a letter و; in either case surmounted by a hèmzè sign; thus, بِئْسَ bïʼsà, بُؤْسَى bùʼsà.

Such disguised medial hèmzè may be followed by a long vowel letter; as, فُؤَاد fùʼād, مَسْؤُول mèsʼūl, رَئِيس rèʼīs. If the hèmzè be changed into a ى figure, and be followed by a long vowel ا, it becomes changed in Turkish, and sometimes in Arabic, into a consonant ى; as in رِيَاسَت rïyāsèt (for رِئَاسَت rïʼāsèt).

There is a striking peculiarity in certain Turkish Ottoman derivatives, which causes great embarrassment to students, and has filled continental Turkish dictionaries and grammars

D

with totally misguiding examples and rules of pronunciation, with regard to the interchangeable vowel-letters و and ى. The peculiarity arose, I imagine, when all Ottoman Turkish was provincial, and was governed by the pronunciation of Asia Minor, variously modified in its various provinces. Thus the earliest writers made use, in all such derivative words, of the vowel-letter و (when they used any at all). They, therefore, wrote گَلُوبْ gėlůb, گِدُوبْ gĭdůb, قَاجُوبْ qâchůb, قِرُوبْ qĭrůb, قُورُوبْ qůrůb; and بَاشْلُو bâshlů, اَلْلُو ėllů; &c. These derivatives became, in course of time, in Europe, and in Constantinople, modified in pronunciation into gėlĭb, gĭdĭb, qâchĭb, qĭrĭb, qůrůb, bâshlĭ, ėlll, &c. The orthography, how-ever, has remained sacred, excepting in the case of provincials, who sometimes write, as they pronounce, گَلِیبْ, گِیدِیبْ, قَاجِیبْ, اَلْلِی, بَاشْلِی, قُورُوبْ, قِیرِیبْ, &c. This subject will be further developed in the paragraphs on Euphony.

Proceed we now to the phonetic values of the consonants.

The letter ب, equally used in Ottoman words of Arabic, Persian, Turkish, and foreign origin, has the value of our *b* generally, whether it be initial, medial, or final in a word. Thus : بَدْ bėd, بِرْ bĭr, بَارْ bâr, بِیزْ bīz, بُوزْ bůz, bŭz, bŭz, bŏz ; اَرِیبْ rĭbât, رَبْطْ rãbt, ثُبُوتْ sůbůt; كِتَابْ kĭtâb, جَنُوبْ jėnůb, عِرِیبْ ėrĭb, حَرْبْ hãrb, قَلْبْ qãlb ; &c. But when medial or final, ending a syllable or word, it sometimes, anomalously, takes the value of our *p*. Thus it is common to hear, كِتَاب kltāp, طُوبْ tóp, ابتدا lptldā, كِتَابْجِى kltāpjl. Especially is this the case with the gerunds in وبْ; as, گِيدُوبْ gldlp, گَلُوبْ gĕllp, يَازُوبْ yázlp, اُوقُويُوبْ óqúyúp, قِيرُوبْ qírlp.

The Persian letter پ is our *p* in all positions: پَدَرْ pĕdĕr, آپَارْ ápár, اِيپْ lp. The Persian word اَسْپ ĕsp, and the Turkish word طُوبْ tóp, are usually written with ب.

The Arabic ت is our *t* in all positions: تَاج tāj, tāj, اَتَلْ ĕtĕl, فَتْوَا fĕtvá, اَتْ ĕt, آتْ át, اِيتْ īt, اُورْت ót. In Turkish grammar it is sometimes changed into movent د in derivatives, when it is originally final and quiescent; as, دُرْت dúrt, دُرْدُنْجُى dúrdúnjú, دُرْدُنْ dúrdún, دُردَه dúrdĕ, دُرُدُى dúrdú, دُردُمْ dúrdúm, &c.; اِيت lt, اِيدَرْ ldĕr, اِيدُوبْ ldlp, اِيدِيجِى ldljl; گِيتْ glt, گِيدَرْ gldĕr, گِيدُوبْ gldlp, گِيدِيجِى gldljl; &c.

The Arabic ث is found in Arabic words only, and in a very few borrowed from the Greek. Its original value is that of our *th* in *think*; so that آيَاثُولُوغْ āyá-thūlūg, for ἅγιος θεολόγος, was not as bad as our *bishop* for ἐπίσκοπος. But in Turkish and Persian this value is unknown; the letter is pronounced as our *s* (sharp, never *z*); áyá-súlūg is therefore the Turkish name of Ephesus, ثَابِتْ is pronounced sāblt, اَثَرْ ĕsĕr, اَحْدَاثْ lhdás, &c. In some Arabic-speaking countries this letter has become a *t*; as, ثَلَاثَ tálátá, &c.

The Arabic ج in Turkish is our *soft g*, which we represent

by a *j* in all positions cf all words, whatever their origin. Thus, جِنْس jĭns, أَجْنَاس ǎjnās, آغَاج āghǎj. In some Arabic-speaking countries it is pronounced like our *hard g*; as, مَسْجِد mĕsgĭd, سَجْدَه sĕgdǎ, &c. Sometimes it takes the sharp sound of چ, q.v.

The Persian چ has the value of our *ch* in *church*, of our *tch* in *crutch*. We never use the latter orthography in our trans-literations,—always the former; as, أَجْمَق ǎchmǎq, چَام chǎm, چُورَك chǔrĕk, چُورُوك chǔrǔk, چُورْبَا chŏrbǎ, ایچ ĭch, چَك chĕk, چِیچَك chĭchĕk. In Turkish derivation, this letter, in Turkish or foreign (not Persian, and there are no Arabic) words, sometimes becomes Arabic ج, but not as a rule.

The Arabic ح has the harshly aspirated sound of our *h* in *horse, hurl, her*; not its soft sound, as heard in *head, him, half*, &c. It is chiefly used in Arabic words; as, حَسَن hǎsǎn, حُسَين hǔsĕyn, فَتَّاح fĕttǎh, جُرْح jǔrh. We represent it by *h*; some adopt *ḥ*, to distinguish it from ه, q.v. Aspirate it always.

The Arabic خ has no equivalent in our language. It is the counterpart of the Scotch and German *ch* in *loch, ich*, &c. It is generally transliterated *kh*, as in the present treatise. Until the student has learnt its true pronunciation, he should con-sider it as a variety of *h*, and never pronounce it as a *k*, especially when it is initial. Thus خِدِیو khĭdīv (pronounce hĭdīv, not kĭdīv), خَدَاوَنْدْگَار khǔdǎ..vĕndghyār (pron. hǔdā...),

سَاخْ shākh, اِخْلَامُورْ ١khlāmūr. In Turkish words, this letter is
often used, provincially, for ق, and is itself sometimes pronounced ق. Thus, بَخَالِمْ bâkhâl١m (for بَقَالِمْ bâqâl١m), اَخْتَامْ
âqshâm (for âkhshâm).

The Arabic د is our *d* in all classes of Ottoman words, and
requires no comment, unless it be to repeat that, in the
derivation of *Turkish* words only, it sometimes takes the
place of ت, and is used instead of ط in original words also;
as, كِتْمَكْ g١tmėk, كِدَرْ g١dėr ; طَاغْ, دَاغْ dâgh.

The Arabic ذ, in an Ottoman mouth, is a *z*. It is found in
Arabic words alone. Different Arab communities pronounce
it as our soft *th* in *this*, as a *d*, or as a *z*. The Turk reads,
اَخْذْ âkhz, ذِكْرْ z١kr (*vulg.* z١k١r), مَأْخُوذْ mė‹khūz, بَذْرْ bėzr.

The Arabic ر is our *r* in every position, in all classes of
words : thus, رَأْفَتْ rė‹fėt, بَارْ bār, آرْدْ ârd. There are two
important remarks, however, which it is necessary for the
English student to bear in mind with respect to this, *to him*,
peculiar letter. Firstly, it *must* always be pronounced (never
dropped or slurred over, as we pronounce *part*, pâ‹t) ; and
secondly, the value of the vowel before it in the same syllable
must never be corrupted (as when we pronounce *pot*, pât ;
for, fâr ; *cur*, cûr ; &c.), but always kept pure, as with any
other consonant ; thus, قُورْ qȯr, قُورْ qȗr, سُورْ sȗr, كُورْ gyȗr, &c. ;
پِيرْ p١r, قِيرْ q١r, قِيرْ qȋr ; &c.

The Arabic ز is our *z* in every word and every position; زَاد zād, زِيـر zīr, زُور zòr, zūr, نَـزْد nezd, اَزْ èz, آزْ ằz, āz, اُوزْ ừz; &c.

The Persian ژ is only found in Persian and French words; it is of the value of our *s* in *treasure, pleasure,* and is transliterated *zh*; as, ژَاژْ zhāzh, پَژْمُرْدَه pòzhmừrdò, اَتَامَازُورْ ètà-mázhòr, &c. It is of very rare occurrence.

The Arabic س is a soft *s*, always followed by a soft vowel in all words. It must never be pronounced as *z*; thus, آسَا āsà, قَوْسْ qàvs, سُوزْ sūz, sừz.

The Arabic ش is our *sh*, always; as, شَاد shād, اِيشْ ìsh, نَشْرْ nèshr.

The Arabic ص, in Turkish, is a hard *s*, used in Turkish, and foreign words also, to designate a hard vowel; thus, اُصّ ừss, اَصْمَقْ ằsmầq, صُوصْمَقْ sừsmầq, قِيصْمَقْ qìsmầq. Never read it *z*.

The Arabic ض is very peculiar, being used in Arabic words only. It is generally pronounced as a hard *z* in Turkish, but sometimes as a hard *d*; thus, رَاضِی rāzì, قَضَا qàzā, اَنْقَاضْ ènqāz; قَاضِی qādì, قَاضِی الْعَسْكَرْ qāzl-'l-ằskèr (vulg. قَاضِی عَسْكَرْ qầz'-'à-kèr), &c. Its Arabic sound is inimitable to a European without long practice.

The Arabic ط, besides being an element of Arabic words, always as a hard *t*, is used in Turkish and foreign words, sometimes with that value, sometimes as a very hard *d*, when

initial. Thus, طُلُوع túlū', قُطْر qútr, خَطّ khátt; طَانْلُو tátlí, طَاغ
dágh, طُوز túz, طِیقَامَتِی tíqámáq, طَاوْرَانْمَتِی dávránmáq.

The Arabic ظ is used in Arabic words only, as a very hard
z. Thus, ظَالِم zálim, ظُلْم zúlm, ظِفْر zífr, ظَفَر záfér, حَظّ házz,
مَحْظُوظً máhzúz.

The Arabic ع is, as a general rule, used in Arabic words
only. It is a strong guttural convulsion in an Arab throat,
softened in Turkish to a *hiatus*, and often disappearing entirely.
We represent it by a Greek *spiritus asper*. Thus, عَصْر 'ásr,
طَعْن tá'n, مَلْعُون mél'ūn, قَطْع qát', مَقْطُوع máqtū'. The Turkish
word عَرَبَ 'áràbà (for أَرَابَه) is, however, with its derivatives,
always written with this letter, of course corruptly.

The Arabic غ is, originally, a peculiar Arabian kind of
hard g, with a sound vergeing on that of the French *r grasséyé*,
which English dandies sometimes imitate. But in Turkish
pronunciation it is either a simple *hard g*, when initial; as,
غَالِب gálib, غَفَلَت gáflét, غَایْدَه gáydá, &c.; and either that when
medial or final in Arabic words only, or like our softened *gh*
in Turkish words; often disappearing, or nearly so, and
changing, like it, into a *w* sound after or before an útárá
hard vowel. Thus, اغْفَال ígfál, صَدْغ sádg, مَغْفُور mágfúr; آغْلَامَتِی
ághlámáq, طَاغ dágh, أُوْلَدِیغِی óldúwú, صُوغَان sówán, طُوغَان dówán,
صُوغُوق sówúq; طَاغُوق táwúq, لَاغُوطَه láwútá; &c.

The Arabic ف is our *f* in all words and all positions.

There is no reason whatever to write the senseless, false Latin-French *ph* instead of *f*, as in *caliph*, a corruption of khálifè, خَلِيفَه. Thus, فَرْض fárz, لَفْظ láfz, صُوف sóf.

The Arabic ق is our *q* in all words and all positions. It is erroneous and regrettable to represent it by *k*, as is generally done. The words قُرْآن qúráän, آق áq, وَقْت wáqt, are thus correctly rendered, leaving the *k* to represent its legitimate ancestor, ك.

The Arabic ك, in all words and all positions, is our *k*. When initial in a word or syllable before a long ا or و vowel, and also before a short útúrú vowel, it borrows, in an Ottoman mouth, the sound of a *y* after itself before the vowel; but not so before the short üstün, the short ésèrè, or the long i vowel. Thus, كَاذِبْ kyázíb, أَكُولْ ékyül, كُوپَكْ kyüpék; كَدِى kédí, كِرَامْ kírám, وَكِيلْ vékíl. Its name, in Arabic, requires no addition; but in Persian and Turkish it has to be distinguished from the Persian letter of the same form, but widely different phonetic value. It is then termed كَاف عَرَبِيَّه kyáfi 'árébíyyé. In Arabic and Persian Ottoman words it remains unchangeable by grammatical inflexion; but in Turkish words, when final, it undergoes phonetic degradation on becoming movent, and is pronounced as a Persian گ, and even as a *y*; or sometimes as a *w* after an útúrú vowel. Thus, اِيپَكْ ípék, اِيپَكَ ípéyé, اِيپَكْن ípéyín, اِيپَكِى ípéyí; سُولُنْ súlún.

sûlûk, سُولُوكَكْ sûlûyûñ, سُولُوكَ sûlûyė, سُولُوكى sûlûyû; اِتَمَكْ
ltmėk, اِتْمَكِينْ ltmėyln.

The Persian گ, called كَانِ فَارِسِيَّه kyâfl fârlslyyė, and
كَانِ فَارِسِى kyâfl fârlsî, or كَانِ عَجَمِى kyâfl 'âjâmî (vulg.
'âjâm kâfl), is the Persian *hard g*. It is unknown in Arabic,
is unchangeable in Persian words, and is never final in
Turkish words or syllables. Thus, سَكْ sėg, سَكِكْ sėglñ,
سَكَ sėgė, سَكى sėgl; كَلْ gâl. In ordinary writing and print
it is undistinguished from its Arabic original; but the Persians
mark it with a double dash: گُلْ gyâl, سَگْ sėg. In some
Turkish books it is marked with three dots: سَكْ, كَلْ.

The Ottoman ى, ignored by all previous writers, eastern
and western, consequently nameless, but which we venture
to term كَانِ عُثْمَانِيَّه kyâfl 'ôsmânlyyė, the Ottoman ى, is
found in Turkish words only, as a medial or a final, never
as an initial to a word, though it is used as an initial letter in
a non-initial syllable. Its phonetic value is that of our *y* in
all cases, though it has no mark to distinguish it. It is both
radical, as in بَكْ bėy, دِكِلْ dlyll, يِكِرْمِى ylylrml; or it is grammatical, declensional, servile, representing a softened Arabic
radical or servile ى, become movent, as in كُوپَكْ kyûpėk,
كُوپَكِكْ kyûpėylñ, كُوپَكَ kyûpėyė, كُوپَكى kyûpėyl; سُورْمَكْ
sûrmėk, سُورْمَكِينْ sûrmėyln; سَوْدِكْ sâvdlk, سَوْدِيكِمْ sâvdlylm,
سَوْدِيكِكْ sâvdlylñ, سُودِيكى sâvdlyl. Most European writers

represent this value by *gà;* but the practice is insufficiently considered, and altogether misleading.

The Ottoman *nasal* ك, distinguished by the name of *surd n*, صَاغِرْ نُون sághir nūn, is a second special Turkish phonetic value of the letter ك, or nasal letter, which we transliterate with the Spanish nasal ñ. It has the phonetic value of our English *ng* nasal, as in *sing, thing,* &c. In ordinary writing and print, it has no mark by which a student may recognize it; but sometimes three dots distinguish it, and one recent writer has marked it with one dot, ڭ (as with him the three dots, ڭ, serve to point out the Persian letter or sound). This value is never initial to a word. As a medial, it sometimes ends, sometimes begins a syllable; as, آكَلَامَق áñlámáq (*vulg.* ánná-máq), تَڭكُرِى táñrí (*vulg.* tárí); كُوكَل gyúñúl, دَكِزْ déñiz, آكِيزْ áñiz, مُوكَرَه sóñrá (*vulg.* sórá). When final to a word, it is usually sounded as a simple *n*; as, بَك béñ (bén), سَنِكْ sáníñ (sánín), كَلِكْ gálíñ (gálín), طَاك dáñ (dán), مُوكْ sóñ (són). When medially final it is usually softened in like manner, or is elided in pronunciation. In آكَلَامَق and its derivates (itself derived from آكَ áñ), the following ل is exceptionally incorporated with it in pronunciation, as though by a kind of inversion of the Arabic rule of conversion for the ل of the definite article ال before certain letters called *solar* (for which see next paragraph on letter ل).

The Arabic ل is our letter *l* in all words and all positions;

as, لُزُوم lầzūm, آلِين ầlĭn, دَالْ dầl. The Turkish word آكَلَامَقْ,
mentioned above, is, with its derivatives, a modern Ottoman
exception of the capital; and the Arabic rule for the conversion of the ل of the definite article الْ, in pronunciation,
when followed by a noun or pronoun beginning with a *solar*
letter, حَرْفِ شَمْسِي hầrfĭ shểmsī, into that solar letter reduplicated by a tểshdīd, is a classical exception, peculiar to Arabic
compounds. The *solar* letters are fourteen in number (exactly
the half of the alphabet); viz., ت, ث, د, ذ, ر, ز, س, ش, ص,
ض, ط, ظ, ل, ن. Thus we have اَلتِّين ểt-tĭn, اَلثَّمَنْ ểs-sểmển,
اَلسُّمن ểs-sümn, اَلدُّعَا ểd-dü'ā, اَلذِّكْرْ ểz-zĭkr, اَلسَّمَكْ ểs-sểmểk,
اَلشَّمْسْ ểsh-shểms (whence the name of شَمْسِي), اَلصَّفَا ểs-sầfâ,
اَلفَّحَا ểd-dühầ, ểz-zühầ, اَلطَّالِعْ ểt-tầlĭ', اَلظُّلْمْ ểz-zülm, اَللَّازِمْ ểl-
lāzĭm, اَلنُّورْ ển-nūr. In the pronoun اَلَّذِى, and its derivatives,
the written ل of the article disappears also. The sign ~ placed
over the ل, so omitted in pronunciation, is named vwầsl, وَصْلْ
junction; and is the letter ص of that word, specially modified.

The Arabic letters م and ن are our *m* and *n* respectively, in
all words and positions: مَالْ māl, اَمَلْ ểmểl, بَنِم bểnĭm, نَاظِرْ nāzĭr,
حُزْن hüzn.

The Arabic letter و is sometimes a consonant, sometimes a
vowel. When a consonant, it has the phonetic value of our *v*,
of our *w*, or of these two combined, the *v* beginning, and the
w ending the sound of the letter. Thus, وَارْ vầr, جَوَابْ jểwāb,

وَصْف vwâsf, وَاقِع vwūqi'. The ear alone can decide these differences. But when the consonant و is reduplicated in an Arabic word, it has always the *v* value; as, أَوَّلْ âvvâl, قَوَّالْ qâvvâl. Ottoman corruption even then may sound it, in hard lettered words, as a reduplicated *w*—qâwwâl. The word قَوَّاف qâwwâf (or قَوَاف qâwâf) is an Ottoman corruption of Arabic خَفَّاف khâffâf.

When the letter و is a vowel in an Arabic or Persian word, it always has the value of ū; excepting a few Persian words, become Ottoman vernaculars, in which it takes the sound of ô. Thus, لُزُومْ lûzūm, مَمْنُونْ mêmnūn; شُورْ shūr; دُوسْتْ dôst (dūst), خُوشْ khôsh (khūsh). In Turkish and foreign words it is generally, if not always, short, and may have either the value of ô, or of ü, û, ŭ, which there is no means of distinguishing, save that of accompanying *hard* or *soft* consonants. With a hard consonant, in a Turkish or foreign word, the vowel-letter و (often omitted) must have the sound of either ô or û, unless it be considered long, when it becomes ō or ū; thus, قُومَقْ qômâq, قُورمَقْ qûrmâq. With a soft consonant, it must be read either ü or û, ū or ū; as, يُوزْمَكْ yüzmêk, سُوزْلُو süzlü. If the accompanying consonant or consonants be neutral, all guidance is lost; as, بُوزْ bôz, būz, bûz, سُوزْ sûz, süz. In derivatives there is, however, frequently a servile vowel or consonant, hard or soft, that helps. Thus, بُوزَانْ bôzân, بُوزُلُوق būzlûlûq, بُوزْمَكْ bûzmêk, سُوزْمَكْ süzmêk; but سُوزْ sûz has no such helping derivative. As to the long and short value, each individual ear must decide for itself in words of these two classes—Turkish and foreign. Vowel و is never initial; it must be preceded by ا to represent an initial ȗtȗrȗ sound; as, اُولْمَقْ ȏlmȃq, اُولَمَكْ ȗlmȇk, &c.

The Arabic letter ا has already been fully discussed.

The Arabic letter ى, like the و, is either a consonant or a vowel.

When a consonant, it has the value of our consonant *y*, whether it be initial, medial, or final, simple or reduplicated. Especially must this be understood when the letter is consonantally final in an Arabic word. As a consonant, and only as a consonant, we transliterate it by a *y*. Therefore, when we use a *y* as the final of a transliterated Arabic word, it must be read and sounded as such, never as an *i* vowel; an observation that continental scholars do not generally understand, unless they may be Germans. Thus we have: يَرْ yȇr, يَدَكْ yȇdȇk, يَازْ yȃz, يُوزْ yȗz, بَيْنْ bȇyn, بُويُونْ bȏyȗn; يَى pȇy, شَى shȇy, رَأَى rȇ'y, مَى mȇy, حَىّ bȃyy, قَيُّومْ qȃyyūm, وَلَى vȇly, رَمَى rȇmy, وَشَى vȇshy, مَشَى mȇshy. This is a difficulty to a student at first, as we have nothing like it in English.

When the ى is a vowel, it is never initial. If a vowel ı or ī sound be initial in any Ottoman word (Arabic, Persian, Turkish, or foreign), the ى, if written, is always preceded by an ۱; as, ایدی ĭdĭ, ایرلامَق ĭrlămăq. When medial, it is always long in Arabic and Persian words; as, اَمیر ĕmīr, بِین bīn. In Turkish and foreign words, medial vowel ی is generally, if not always short; as, ویرمَك vĭrmĕk, قِبرمَق qĭrmăq. When final in an Arabic word, it is also always short; as, قَاضی qāzĭ, رَاضی rāzĭ, دَاعی dā'ĭ, جَاری jārĭ, سَاری sārĭ, &c. But there are hosts of Arabic words ending in reduplicated consonantal ی, which, in Persian and Turkish, are used as Arabic words, generally adjectives, terminating in a long vowel ī or ĭ; as, یَومی yĕvmī, سَنَوی sĕnĕvī, شَهری shĕhrī, عَرَبی 'ărĕbī, فَارِسی fārĭsī, قَطعی qăt'ī, اُفُقی ŭfŭqī, حِفظی hĭfzī, &c. When these become feminine, the reduplicated nature of their final consonantal ی becomes apparent; as, یَومِیَّه yĕvmĭyyĕ, قَطعِیَّه qăt'ĭyyĕ, &c.

There are many Persian derivative words, adjectives or substantives (besides others not used in Turkish), which really end in long vowel ی. The adjectives are precisely similar to the Arabic adjectives just described, as modified in Persian and Turkish; but they have no feminine. Thus, شَاهی shāhī, 'royal;' خُسرَوی khŭsrĕvī, 'imperial;' شِیرَازی shīrāzī, 'of Shiraz;' &c. The substantives indicate abstract qualities; as, شَاهی shāhī, 'royalty;' وَزِیری vĕzīrī, 'vezirial office or functions;' &c.

Turkish and foreign final ی, radical or servile, is always a short vowel; as, كَدی kĕdĭ, آری ărĭ, &c.; اَوی ĕvĭ, بَابَاسِی băbă-sĭnĭ, اُوطَهبِی ŏdăyĭ, تَرَبِی tĕrĕyĭ, &c.

The vowels ا and ى are sometimes interchangeable in Turkish words and derivations, and are sometimes omitted, without any inflexible rule being assignable. Thus, ايتْمَامَكْ, ايتْمَمَكْ, ايتْمَمَكْ, itmèmèk, are all admissible. The true rule is: "Never introduce a vowel letter into a Turkish or foreign word without removing a possible doubt as to pronunciation ; never leave out a vowel in such word, if by the omission a doubt is created as to pronunciation." The orthography of Arabic and Persian words is fixed, and admits of no such variation. Persian words admit, however, of abbreviation by the omission of a vowel ; as, شَاه shāh, شَه shèh ; پَادْشَاه pādshāh (*vulg.* pādishāh), پَادْشَه pādshèh ; شَاهِنْشَاه shāhìnshāh, شَاهِنْشَه shāhìnshèh, شَهِنْشَاه shèhìnshāh, شَهِنْشَه shèhìnshèh ; &c.

In many Turkish words the vowels و and ى are used for one another by different writers, at different times, in different places; even at one place and time ; even by one writer at different times, or in the selfsame document ; but this last as a license or an inadvertency. Consistency in this matter is advisable. Thus we have: بَاشْلُو bàshlù, بَاشْلِي bàshlì, كُورُ gèlùr, كَيِر gèlìr ; آرُو àrù, آرى àrì ; &c.; words differently written, but the selfsame in reality.

The Ottoman alphabet is divided into three classes of consonants, hard, soft, and neutral. The hard letters are nine in number : ق , غ , ع , ظ , ط , ض , ص , خ , ح . The soft letters are only six : أ , ت , ز , س , ك , ه . The remaining letters, sixteen in the whole, are neutral : ب , پ , ت , ج , چ , د , ذ , ر , ژ , ش , ف , ل , م , ن , و , ی .

As the orthography of every Arabic and Persian Ottoman word is fixed and unchangeable, it is only in Turkish and foreign Ottoman words, and in the declensions and conjugations of all Ottoman words, that the rules relating to hard and soft letters are carried out. This is the first and chief part of the beautiful system of Ottoman euphony.

If any one of the hard or soft consonants is used in a Turkish Ottoman word, all the other radical and servile letters of the word, of its derivations, and of its declension or conjugation, must be of the same class, or of the neuters. Thus we have: قازمق qâzmâq, كزمك gèzmèk ; قازدیغی qâzdîghî, كزدیكی gèzdîyî ; قارلق qârlîq, كوزلك gyûzlûk ; &c.

The Ottoman vowels are also of these three classes. The hard vowels are : â, ā, î, ī, ó, ō, û, ū ; eight in all. The soft vowels also eight : â, è, î, ī, û, ū, û, ū. The neutral vowels are â, ā, â. These vowels always accompany their own class of consonants, or the neutrals. The neutral vowels can accompany any class of consonant. Thus we have : بابا bâbâ, انا ânâ, پاشا pâshâ, سن sân, بن bèn, قیرمق qîrmâq, كیرمك gîrmèk, قومق qômâq, قورمق qûrmâq, كوزتمك gyûzètmèk, كورمك gyûrmèk.

When in a Turkish Ottoman word a vowel is the dominant letter, its consonant or consonants being neutrals, the declension, conjugation, and derivation from that word follow the class to which the dominant vowel belongs; thus, آتْمَق åtmåq, اَغِرْلِق åghirlìq, اِيرْلَمَق irlåmåq, اُومْمَق åmmåq, اُوغْرَامَق óghråmåq; اَلَمَكْ élémék, اِينْمَكْ inmék, يُوزْمَكْ yåzmék, اُورْمَكْ årmék.

When an Arabic or Persian word is declined or derived from, in Ottoman Turkish, its last dominant letter or vowel decides whether the declension or derivation shall be made with hard or soft letters and vowels; thus, مَرْبُوطْ mérbūt, مَرْبُوطْلِق mérbūtlåq; اَمِيرْ émīr, اَمِيرْلِكْ émīrlìk; آسَانْ āsān, آسَانْلِق āsānlìq; &c.

When the sole dominant vowel of a Turkish Ottoman word, or the last dominant letter or vowel of a Turkish, Arabic, Persian, or foreign Ottoman word, is of the *o* or *u* class, hard or soft, all possible consonants, and all vowels in the declension, conjugation, or derivation therefrom, not only conform to the class of such dominant, but furthermore, all consecutive servile vowels in the derivatives that would otherwise be éséré, become åtårå, of the class of the dominant; that is, become å when the dominant is ó or å, and become å when the dominant is å or å; thus, اُولْدِى ólgån, اُولْغِينْلِق ólgånlåq, اُولْدِى óldå; طُوتْغِينْ tåtgån, طُوتْغِينْلِق tåtgånlåq, طُوتْدِى tåtdå; سُورُوكْدُرْمَكْ såråkdårmék, سُورُوكْدُرُلْمَكْ såråkdårålmék; سُورُشْمَكْ såråshmék, سُورُشْدُرْمَكْ såråshdårmék, سُورُشْدُرُلْمَكْ såråshdårålmék; كُورُشْمَكْ gyåråshmék, كُورُشْدُرْمَكْ gyåråshdårmék, كُورُشْدُرُلْمَكْ gyåråshdårålmék.

E

gyúrúshdúrúlmék. But if, in such words, an ústún vowel come in by the ordinary course of derivation or conjugation, and be followed by a syllable or syllables with an éséré vowel, the influence of the radical dominant útúrú is destroyed by such intervention; as, بوزُشَمَقْ bózúshmáq, بوزُشْمَقْلِق bózúshmáqlíq, بوزُشْمَغِين bózúshmághín; كُورُشْمَكْ gyúrúshmék, كُورُشْمَكْلِكْ gyúrúshméklík, كُورُشْمَكِين gyúrúshméyín.

CHAPTER II.

THE OTTOMAN ACCIDENCE OR ETYMOLOGY.

SECTION I. *The Noun Substantive.*

THERE is no gender. If the female of an animal has not a special name, as, طَاوُق (tàwùq), *a hen*, قِسْرَاق (qìsràq), *a mare*, اِيَنَك (ìnèk), *a cow*, قَانْجِق (qànjìq), *a bitch*, the female is named, as with us, *a she...*, دِيشِى (dìshì); as, دِيشِى أَرْسْلَان (dìshì àrslàn), *a lioness; &c.* If the female be a girl or woman, she is never named dìshì, but is mentioned as قِيز (qìz), *maiden*, or قَارِى (qàrì), *matron*, accordingly; as, قِيزخِذْمَتْجِى (qìz khìzmètjì), or خِذْمَتْجِى قِيز (khìzmètjì qìz), *a servant maid, a maidservant;* قَارِى آشْجِى (qàrì àshjì), or آشْجِى قَارِى (àshjì qàrì), *a woman cook, a cook woman.*

There is, really, no declension of nouns in Turkish; but the prepositions, perhaps eight in number, by some termed *postpositions*, are subjoined to the noun, singular or plural, the plural being always formed by adding the syllable لَرْ (làr, lèr) to the singular; thus:

Nom.	أُوق òq	*(arrow)*,	أُوقْلَرْ òqlàr	*(arrows)*.
Gen.	أُوقُكْ òquñ	*(of —)*,	أُوقْلَرِكْ òqlàrìn	

Dat.	اوقه óqǎ	(to —),	اوقلره óqlǎrǎ.	
Loc.	اوقده óqdǎ	(in —),	اوقلرده óqlǎrdǎ.	
Acc.	اوقى óqù	(the —),	اوقلرى óqlǎrî.	
Abl.	اوقدن óqdǎn	(from —),	اوقلردن óqlǎrdǎn.	
Inst.	اوقله óqlǎ	(with —),	اوقلرله óqlǎrlǎ.	
Caus.	اوق ايچون óq íchùn	(for —),	اوقلر ايچون óqlǎr íchùn.	

Nom.	او év (house),		اولر évlér (houses).	
Gen.	اوڭ évíñ,		اولرڭ évléríñ.	
Dat.	اوه évé,		اولره évléré.	
Loc.	اوده évdé,		اولرده évlérdé.	
Acc.	اوى évî,		اولرى évlérî.	
Abl.	اودن évdén,		اولردن évlérdén.	
Inst.	اوله évlé,		اولرله évlérlé.	
Caus.	او ايچون év íchùn,		اولر ايچون évlér íchùn.	

Most Turkish singulars (not all) ending in ت soften this
letter into د before a junctional vowel preposition ; thus, قورت
(qùrt), *wolf,* قوردڭ qùrdùñ, قورده qùrdǎ, قوردى qùrdù ; not so
before a consonant or separate word ; as, قورتله ,قورتدن ,قورتده,
قورت ايچون ; but آتڭ átíñ, اوتى ótù, &c.

Most, if not all, Turkish singulars, of more than one
syllable, ending in ق, soften it into غ before junctional
vowels ; as, چارداق (chǎrdǎq), *trellis,* چارداغڭ chǎrdǎghíñ,

جَارْدَاغَ chárdágh, جَارْدَاغِى chárdághi. Those in Arabic ك
soften it into Turkish ك (*y* value); اِيـپَكْ (ípék), *silk*, اِيـپَكِ
(ípéylñ), اِيـپَكَ (ípéyé), اِيـپَـى (ípéyí). Those in Persian ك (*g*
value), do not change it; as, سَنْكْ séng, *stone*, سَنْكِكْ (séngíñ),
سَنْكَ (séngé), سَنْكِى (séngí).

These rules do not apply to Arabic and Persian substantives; these retain their final ى or ك unchanged; unless the
borrowed word has passed into the mouth of the vulgar as an
everyday expression; as, فِسْتِق fístíq, فِسْتِغِنْ fístíghín, &c.

Singulars ending in a vowel, take ن in the genitive, and
consonant ى in the dative and accusative, to support the
vowel taken by a final consonant; as, بَابَا (bábá), *father*, بَابَانِكْ
(bábáníñ), بَابَايَ (bábáyá), بَابَايِى (bábáyí); قَپُو (qápú), *door, gate*,
قَپُونُكْ (qápúnúñ), قَپُويَ (qápúyá), قَپُويِى (qápúyú, where útúrú
dominates); آرِى (árí), *bee*, آرِينِكْ (áríníñ), آرِييَ (áríyá, written
separately on account of two letters ى), آرِييِى (áríyí); كَدِى
(kédí), *cat*, كَدِينِكْ (kédíníñ), كَدِييَ (kédíyé), كَدِييِى (kédíyí), &c.

Singulars ending in vowel ه do not join this letter to the
sign of the plural, in writing; as, پِيدَه (pídé), پِيدَەلَرْ (pídélér).

The word صو (sú), *water*, irregularly forms its genitive as
صُويُكْ (suyúñ, almost the only exception or irregularity in the
language). صُوى (sóy), *sort*, ends in a consonant, and is regular;
صُويُكْ (sóyúñ), صُويَه (sóyá), صُويِى (sóyú).

Arabic and Persian substantives never change their final consonants for declension; طَبَق (tâbâq), *plate*, طَبَقِن tâbâqîñ; اِمْسَاك (ímsāk), *refraining*, اِمْسَاكَه (ímsākė); صَلَاتْ (sâlāt), *worship*, صَلَاتِى (sâlātí). Their final vowels follow the same rules with those in Turkish words; دُعَا (dâ'ā), *prayer*, دُعَانَكْ dâ'ânîñ); بِيَادَه (píyādė), *foot-man*, بِيَادَيَه (píyādėyė); چَارْسُو chārsū), *market*, چَارْسُويِى (chārsūyù); ثُلَاثِى (sûlāsī), *triliteral root*, ثُلَاثِىِى (sûlāsīyí).

They form their plurals as Turkish words; but Persian names of men and their kinds use the Persian plural also, if judged proper. This is formed by adding an ûstûn vowel, followed by ان, to the final consonant of the singular; as, مَرْدْ (mèrd), *man*, مَرْدَانْ (mèrdān). If the singular ends in ه vowel, it is changed into consonant گ (Persian), with ûstûn vowel, before the ان of the plural; as, خَوَاجَه (kh'ājė), *master*, خَوَاجَگَانْ (kh'ājėgyān). Singulars ending in vowel و take consonant ى instead of گ; as, خُوبْرُو (khūb-rū), *a beauty in face*, خُوبْرُويَانْ (khūb-rūyān). Those ending in vowel ى change it into consonant ى in like manner; as, سِپَاهِى (sípāhī), *man-at-arms*, سِپَاهِيَانْ (sípāhíyān). [Persian writers explain this by saying: "The final long vowel is in reality two letters ى rolled into one. One of these is now used as a consonant."] Other Persian substantives form the plural by adding the syllable هَا hā; as, نَانْهَا (nān-hā), *loaves, breads*, أَسْبْهَا (èsb-hā), *horses*.

Arabic plurals, of the regular forms for men and women, and of the various irregular forms for these and other things, and also thé Arabic duals, are used in Turkish. The dual is formed by adding ûstûn followed by اَن (ān) in the nominative, which becomes يَن (èyn) in the oblique case. The latter is frequently used in Turkish as a nominative; as, قُطْب (qùtb), pole, قُطْبَان (qùtbān), قُطْبَيْن (qùtbèyn), *the two poles.*

The regular plural masculine nominative for *men* is formed by adding ûtûrû followed by وِن (ūn) to the singular. This becomes ésèré followed by يِن (in) in the oblique case, also used as a nominative in Turkish; the plural feminine is with ûstûn followed by اَت (āt) in all cases; thus, مُسْلِم (mùslìm), a *Muslim,* مُسْلِمُون (mùslìmūn), مُسْلِمِين (mùslìmīn), مُسْلِمَات (mùslìmāt), *Muslims.*

The irregular Arabic plurals commonly used in Turkish are of rather numerous forms, and there are many more plural forms used occasionally. These irregular plural Arabic forms are not obtained by adding a letter or letters, vowel or consonant, to the end of the singular, but by varying the vowel or vowels of the word, and by adding letters, consonant or vowel, as the case may be, before, between, or after, the letters of the singular. To enable the student to obtain a fair insight into this very intricate but beautiful system, I have to say, first of all, that a paradigm has been adopted by Arabian grammarians, according to which all such modifications may be effected. They have taken the triliteral فَعَل (fâ'âlâ) as the representative of any and every triliteral root-word, and they have modified this root into every shape that can, under any circumstances, be taken by any derivative of any triliteral root in the language. All those modifications, when not made on the vowels alone of the triliteral, are effected by adding *servile letters*, or *a servile letter*, here and there, before, after, and in the midst of, the three radical consonants, with appropriate mutations, in each case, of the vowels, long or short, in the new word. Thus, to speak only of Arabic nouns, substantive or adjective, used in Turkish, we have, in the first place, to learn the *forms* of their singulars (for they all have definite forms), and then the forms of the plurals special to each of these singulars.

To facilitate and systematize this knowledge, the Arabian grammarians have divided the whole language into sections of biliteral, triliteral, quadriliteral, quinqueliteral, &c., roots, which they term, respectively, ثُنَائِى (sûnâ'î), ثُلَاثِى (sûlâsî), رُبَاعِى (rûbâ'î), خُمَاسِى (khûmâsî), سُدَاسِى (sûdâsî), &c. These are the Turkish pronunciations of the terms. I do not remember ever to have seen or heard the expression أَحَادِى (ûhâdî), which would be the analogous name for uniliteral root; but it may perhaps be found. Of these, the triliterals form by very far the most important and numerous class, the quadriliterals coming next. These are represented,

respectively, by the supposititious paradigmatic words فَعَلَ
(fa'ălă) and فَعْلَلَ (fă'lĕlĕ).

Every triliteral root is theoretically capable of giving rise
to fifteen chapters of derivation, called بَابْ (bāb, *pl.* أَبْوَابْ
ĕbvāb). These chapters are respectively termed : 1, فَعَلْ بَابِى
(fă'ălă bābĭ), *the chapter of the triliteral* ; 2, تَفْعِيلْ بَابِى (tĕf'īl
bābĭ), *the chapter of* (the verbal noun) تَفْعِيلْ ; 3, مُفَاعَلَه بَابِى
(mŭfā'ălĕ băbĭ) ; 4, تَفَعُّلْ بَابِى (tĕfă'ŭl —); 5, اِنْفِعَالْ بَابِى (lf'āl bābĭ) ;
6, تَفَاعُلْ بَابِى (tĕfā'ŭl —) ; 7, اِنْفِعَالْ بَابِى (lnfl'āl —); 8, اِفْتِعَالْ بَابِى
(lftl'āl —); 9, اِنْعِلَالْ بَابِى (lf'īlāl —); 10, اِسْتِفْعَالْ بَابِى (lstlf'āl —);
11, اِفْعِوَّالْ بَابِى (lf'īlāl —); 12, اِفْعِيعَالْ بَابِى (lf'ī'āl —); 13, اِفْعِيلَالْ بَابِى
(lf'īvvāl —); 14, اِفْعِنْلَالْ بَابِى (lf'ĭnlāl —); 15, اِفْعَنْلَى بَابِى (lf'ĭnlă —).
The use of words from the last four chapters is next to
unknown in Turkish, if not quite so ; and the use of chapters
9 and 11, اِفْعِيلَالْ, اِفْعِلَالْ, is confined to the expression of
colours, the second expressing an *intensity of degree.* All the
other nine chapters of derivation are constantly met with in
Turkish, as nouns, substantive and adjective. Occasionally,
even a verb is used ; but as a kind of invocatory interjection.
All but the first of these names (which is the form of three
out of the six varieties of its verb) is the form of one of the
verbal nouns, or of the sole verbal noun, connected with the
verb of the chapter ; and each chapter has two adjectives

deriving from it, the active and passive participles of the verb of the chapter. The first, or triliteral, chapter possesses, furthermore, several other special forms of nouns deriving from its verb other than its verbal nouns (which are a kind of infinitive, or noun of action or being, corresponding with our English substantive form in -*ing*, as, *walking, singing, cutting, suffering, lasting*, &c., as acts or states). Of these, I give here merely those frequently met with in Turkish ; and it must be understood, that in this simple triliteral chapter, the various forms of verbal nouns are never all found deriving from one verb ; but certain forms belong to one or more kinds of tri-literal verbs, others to other kinds. These *kinds* of verbs, again, are of two sorts ; there are verbs transitive or active, and there are verbs intransitive or neuter ; and certain verbal nouns are more used than others with each of these two kinds. Again, there are the six conjugations of this simple triliteral chapter ; and each conjugation has its preferential form or forms of verbal noun. The Turkish Qāmūs dictionary dilates on this subject more than other works, and much information can be obtained from it, in addition to what should be studied in the " Grammar of the Arabic Language," by Dr. Wm. Wright, vol. i., p. 109, par. 196, where 36 forms of " *nomina verbi* " are given for this triliteral chapter alone, and several others may be found in De Sacy's " Grammaire Arabe," 2nd edition, 1831, vol. i., p. 283, par. 629. Those that are principally used in Turkish are the following: 1, فَعْل (fä'l); 2, فَعَل (fä'àl); 3, فِعْل (fi'l); 4, فُعْل (fu'l); their feminines: 5, فَعْلَـه (fä'lè); 6, فَعَلَه (fä'àlè); 7, فِعْلَه (fi'lè); 8, فُعْلَه (fu'lè); the same forms, with an insititious or servile long vowel ا: 9, فَعَال (fä'âl); 10, فِعَال (fi'âl); 11, فُعَال (fu'âl); and their feminines: 12, فَعَالَه (fä'âlè); 13, فِعَالَه (fi'âlè); 14, فُعَالَه (fu'âlè); some of the same, with long vowel و or ى; and their feminines: 15, فَعُول (fä'ûl); 16, فُعُول (fu'ûl); 17, فَعِيل (fä'îl); 18, فَعُولَه (fä'ûlè); 19, فُعُولَه (fu'ûlè); 20, فَعِيلَه (fä'îlè); the same, with final servile ان added: 21, فَعَلَان (fä'lân); 22, فِعْلَان (fi'lân); 23, فُعْلَان (fu'lân); the special feminine form: 24, فَعَالِيَت (fä'âliyèt); and the special forms in initial servile م, with their feminines: 25, مَفْعَل (mèf'àl); 26, مَفْعِل (mèf'il); 27, مَفْعَلَه (mèf'àlè); 28, مَفْعِلَه (mèf'ilè); with the two special forms in initial servile ت, with long vowel ا intercalated: 29, تَفْعَال (tèf'âl); 30, تِفْعَال (tif'âl). Many original substantives and adjectives are of one or other of the forms here given; and in frequent cases it is disputed whether such words are substantives or verbal nouns. The active participle, *nomen agentis*, of this chapter is: 31, فَاعِل (fâ'il); 32, feminine, فَاعِلَـه (fâ'ilè); and the passive participle, *nomen patientis*, is: 33, مَفْعُول (mèf'ûl); 34, feminine, مَفْعُولَه (mèf'ûlè); derivative adjectives are met with, branches of this chapter, as: 35, فَعْل (fä'l); 36, فَعِل (fä'il); 37, فَعُول (fä'ûl; often feminine); 38, فَعِيل (fä'îl); and the feminine of this last: 39, فَعِيلَه (fä'îlè);

the diminutive, substantive or adjective: 40, فُعَيْل (fû'êyl); the noun of unity: 41, فَعْلَه (fâ'lè); the noun of kind or manner: 42, فِعْلَه (fï'lè); the noun of place and time: 43, مَفْعَل méf'âl; sometimes méf'îl and مَفْعَلَه méf'âlè); the noun of the place of abundance: 44, مَفْعَلَه (méf'êlè); the noun of instrument and receptacle: 45, مِفْعَل (mïf'âl; sometimes مِفْعَال mïf'âl, and مِفْعَلَه mïf'âlè; rarely مُفْعُل mêf'ûl and مُفْعُلَه mûf'ûlè); and others still which need not be classified here, though a knowledge of their special forms and meanings, when acquired, assists greatly to au accurate appreciation of Arabic diction, as occasionally met with in Turkish.

The irregular plurals of these forms mostly met with, when the words are substantives and masculine, are: 1, أَفْعَال (èf'âl); 2, فُعُول (fû'ûl); 3, فِعَال (fï'âl); 4, أَفْعُل (èf'ûl); 5, أَفْعِلَه (èf'îlè); 6, فُعَّال (fû''âl) and 7, فَعَلَه (fâ'âlè; both for the form فاعل (fâ'l); 8, فُعَلَا (fû'âlā) and 9, أَفْعِلَا (èf'îlā; both for the form فعيل fâ'îl); 10, فَعَلَا (fâ'âlā; for the form فَعْلَا fâ'lâ); when they are feminine in form, either; 11, فِعَل (fï'âl; for the form فِعْلَه fï'lè), or 12, فُعَل (fû'âl; for the form فُعْلَه fû'lè), or 13, أَفْعَال (èf'âl; as for masculines); 14, فَعَائِل (fâ'â'il; for the forms فَعَالَه fâ'âlè, فَعُولَه fâ'ûlè فَعِيلَه fâ'îlè); 15, فَوَاعِل (fèvâ'l; for the form فَاعِلَه fâ'âlè); besides 16, مَفَاعِل (méfâ'l; for the forms méf'âl, méf'îl, mïf'âl, and their variants); 17, مَفَاعِيل (méfâ'l; for the forms مِفْعَال, مَفْعُول); and others more rarely used.

Adjectives masculine derived from this triliteral chapter, much used in Turkish, are of the two forms فَعِيل (fâ'îl) and أَفْعَل (éf'âl); feminines, respectively, فَعِيلَه (fâ'île) and فَعْلَا (fâ'lā, for Arabic فَعْلَاء; of أَفْعَل when not comparative) or فُعْلَا (fú'lâ, for Arabic فُعْلَى; of the same أَفْعَل when comparative). The plurals of these are: فُعَلَا (fú'âlā) or أَفْعِلَه (éf'île), for فَعِيل, as in the substantive; and فُعْل (fú'l), for أَفْعَل and its feminines.

We now come to the derived chapters.

The verbal nouns of the second chapter are: تَفْعِيل (téf'îl), تَفْعَال (téf'âl; sometimes tîf'âl), and تَفْعِلَه (téf'île); the plurals of the whole of which are of the form تَفَاعِيل (téfa'îl); though the first makes also a quasi-regular plural, تَفْعِيلَاتْ (téf'î'ât). Its active participle is مُفَعِّل (múfâ"îl, fem. مُفَعِّلَه múfâ"île); and its passive participle is مُفَعَّل (múfâ"âl, fem. مُفَعَّلَه múfâ"âle), of which the masculine is also used as a noun of time and place.

The verbal nouns of the third chapter are: مُفَاعَلَه (múfâ'âlè) and فِعَال (fî'âl; this latter only occasionally used); the active participle is مُفَاعِل (múfâ'îl, fem. مُفَاعِلَه múfâ'île); the passive participle, مُفَاعَل (múfâ'âl, fem. مُفَاعَلَه múfâ'âlè, exactly like the first verbal noun).

The verbal noun of the fourth chapter is أَفْعَال (îf'âl); a. p. مُفْعِل (múf'îl, fem. مُفْعِلَه); p. p. مُفْعَل (múf'âl, fem. مُفْعَلَه).

The fifth chapter has : *v. n.*, تَفَعُّل (tèfǎ"ùl); *a. p.* مُتَفَعِّل (mùtè-fǎ"îl, fem. مُتَفَعِّلَه); *p. p.* مُتَفَعَّل (mùtèfǎ"àl, fem. مُتَفَعَّلَه).

The sixth : *v. n.* تَفَاعُل (tèfà'ùl) ; مُتَفَاعِل (mùtèfà'îl, مُتَفَاعِلَه); مُتَفَاعَل (mùtèfà'àl, مُتَفَاعَلَه).

The seventh : اِنْفِعَال (ìnfì'àl), مُنْفَعِل (mùnfà'îl, مُنْفَعِلَه), (mùnfà'àl, مُنْفَعَلَه).

The eighth : اِفْتِعَال (ìftì'àl), مُفْتَعِل (mùftà'îl, مُفْتَعِلَه), مُفْتَعَل (mùf-tà'àl, مُفْتَعَلَه).

The ninth: اِفْعِلَال (ìf'ìlàl), *a. p.* مُفْعَلّ (mùf'àll, مُفْعَلَّه mùf'àllè); no *p. p.*

The tenth: اِسْتِفْعَال (ìstìf'àl), مُسْتَفْعِل (mùstèf'îl, مُسْتَفْعِلَه), (mùstèf'àl, مُسْتَفْعَلَه).

The eleventh : اِفْعِيلَال (ìf'ìlàl), مُفْعَالّ (mùf'àll, مُفْعَالَّه mùf'àllè) ; no *p. p.*

As to the significations of these chapters, it may be shortly said that when the first is transitive, the second is causative or intensive ; and when the first is intransitive, the second— causative still in the same sense, but not intensive—is tran- sitive. Sometimes the second has the sense, not of making (a thing) do or be (so or so), but of making (it) out to be (so and so), of deeming, judging, pronouncing, or calling (it so and so) ; rarely, it unmakes also.

The third chapter denotes reciprocity of the action between

two, or among several or many agents, or an expected reciprocity when one agent only is shown. Thus, مُكَاتَبَ a *mutually writing letters* (to one another), *a writing in expectation of a reply*; قِنَال *a mutually striving to kill one another, fighting.* When the triliteral is expressive of a state, as حُسْن (húsn), *a being beautiful or good*, the third form expresses an action corresponding with that state in the agent; thus, مُحَاسَنَة (múhásèné), *a doing good, and acting well, kindly to* (the other).

The fourth form is causative, generally, but sometimes intransitive; thus, إِرْسَال (írsál), *a sending* (some person or thing); اِقْبَال (íqbál), *an advancing.*

The fifth form has the sense of acquiring a state, sometimes by one's own act, sometimes through the act of another; as, نَكَسَّر (tékèssúr), *a becoming broken.* This may be transitive at times; as, تَعَلُّم (tá'állúm), *a becoming knowing in* (a science, art, &c.); i. e., *a learning* (it).

The sixth form has the idea of reciprocity, something like the third, but more decided, more certain in fact; thus, تَقَانُل (táqátúl), *a mutually killing one another.* Sometimes it has the sense of feigning a state; as, تَجَاهُل (téjáhúl), *a feigning to be ignorant.* Sometimes, again, it expresses a repeated act; thus, تَقَاضَا (táqázá), *a dunning, repeatedly demanding the fulfilment and discharge* (of some incumbent act or debt).

The seventh and eighth forms, like the fifth, imply the acquisition of a state, either by one's own act, or as the result of the act of another; thus, اِنْفِعَال (Inffäl), *a being acted upon, affected, hurt, wounded, vexed* (by another's act); اِنْتِظَار (intizār) *a* (becoming) *looking forward* (for the occurrence of an event). Sometimes the eighth form is transitive in the sense of *acquiring*; thus, اِفْتِرَاس (iftirās), *an acquiring* (game) *by hunting*; or, a seeking to acquire; as, اِلْتِمَاس (iltimās), *a seeking to obtain* (a favour) *by* (morally) *feeling one's way* (by touching, groping, requesting); *a requesting.*

The ninth and eleventh express two degrees of state as to colour, and sometimes as to defects; the eleventh denoting intensity of that state; thus, اِحْمِرَار (ihmirār), *a being red; redness;* اِحْمِيرَار (ihmīrār), *a being very red;* اِعْوِجَاج (i'vijāj, *a being crooked; crookedness;* اِعْوِيجَاج (i'vījāj), *a being very crooked; anfractuosity.*

The tenth usually expresses *a trying to get* (the act or state signified by the first form); as, اِسْتِفْسَار (istifsār), *an asking for an explanation of* (a matter). Sometimes it has, like the second, the sense of *deeming* or *judging* (a thing) *to be* (what the first form signifies); as, اِسْتِثْقَال (istisqāl), *a deeming* (a person or thing) *heavy, disagreeable, tedious.* And sometimes it means *an acquiring a state,* expressed by the first form; thus, اِسْتِشْفَا (istishfā), *a becoming restored to health.* And again, it

occasionally has the sense of the first form ; as, اِسْتِعْدَاد
(ĭstĭ'dād), *a being or becoming ready prepared ; readiness*
(external or mental); *mental capacity and quickness in acquiring
dexterity or knowledge.*

Quadriliteral roots have but four forms ; of which only two
are perceptibly used in Turkish, the first and second. The
first has two verbal nouns, figured paradigmatically by فَعْلَلَ
(fā'lĕlĕ), and فِعْلَال (fĭ'lāl); the second, but one, figured by
تَفَعْلُل (tĕfā'lŭl); سَلْطَنَت (sălṭănăt) may serve as an instance of
a verbal noun of the first form, and تَسَلْطُن (tĕsălṭŭn) as an
example of the second.

It would occupy too much space to detail here the modifications of these results arising in the case of roots where the
second and third radicals are identical, or of those in which
one, two, or all three of the radicals belong to the trio ا, و, ی,
out of which the long vowels, the *letters of prolongation,*
spring. These details should be studied in Wright's, or in
De Sacy's Arabic Grammar. But it is necessary to remark
that these Arabic verbal nouns belong equally to the active
and passive voice of their verbs; so that, as in English, the
same word, فَتْح fĕt-h for instance, will sometimes mean a *con-
quering,* at others a *being conquered,* just as our word *conquest*
does. This last rule holds good with Persian verbal nouns,
not much used in Turkish. It is not so, however, with
Turkish verbal nouns, excepting, to a slight extent, with the

F

present, as in مه mâ, mè; and this for the simple reason that
every passive Turkish verb has its own special verbal nouns
complete, present, past, and future.

Every Turkish, Persian, and Arabic substantive has its
diminutive, the two latter seldom used in Ottoman phrases.

The Turkish diminutive substantive is formed usually by
suffixing the syllable جِك (jìk) or جِق (jìq) to the word, of
whatever origin, whether it end in a consonant or vowel.
Thus, اَرِيكْجِكْ (èrìkjìk) a *little plum*, اِتْجِكْ (ìtjìk) a *little dog*,
كِتَابْجِكْ (kìtābjìk or كِتَابْجِق kìtâbjìq) a *little book*, كَاتِبْجِكْ (kyātìb-
jìk) a *little clerk*,' دَوَهجِكْ (dèvèjìk) a *little camel*, اُتُوجُكْ (ùtùjùk),
a *little flat-iron*, كَدِيجِكْ (kèdìjìk) a *little cat*, اَلْمَاجِق (èlmâjìq)
a *little apple*, پَاشَاجِق (pâshâjìq) a *little pasha*, پَادِشَاهْجِق (pādì-
shâhjìq) a *little monarch*, قَپُوجُق (qâpùjùq) a *little door or gate*,
خُوَاجَهجِق (khòjâjìq) a *little professor*, قَارِيجِقْ (qârìjìq) a *little
woman*.

In words ending with ك or ق, after a movent consonant, it
would form a cacophony to repeat these letters for the
diminutive. The less important is therefore sacrificed to
euphony, and omitted in the diminutive, a vowel letter usually
taking its place: كُورَكْ (kyùrèk), كُورَهجِكْ (kyùrèjìk), a *little
shovel or oar*; چُوجُق (chòjùq), چُوجُوجُق (chòjùjùq), a *little child*.

This form of the diminutive is sometimes modified into that
of جَكِزْ (jèyìz), جَغِزْ (jâghìz); thus, اَوْجَكِزْ (èvjèyìz) a *little house*,

قِيزْجَغِزْ (qîzjàghîz), *a little girl.* As is seen, the former èsèrè vowel of the ج in the diminutive has now become an ûstûn, as the èsèrè has been passed on to the ك or ی, modified into Turkish ك (*y* value) or غ (soft *gh* value). Euphony requires it.

These diminutives are used as terms of endearment also, exactly as in German, and as our nursery vocabulary says, *daddy, mammy, granny, aunty, doggy, horsey,* &c. ; only, in Turkish, the method is of universal application, by all classes, not by children only.

The Persian diminutive always ends in چَه (chè) ; as, پَا (pā), پَاچَه (pāchè), or in ك preceded by an ûstûn vowel ; as, كَنِيزْ (kènīz), كَنِيزَك (kènīzèk).

The Arabic diminutive also makes its first vowel ûtûrû, and the next vowel ûstûn, followed by a quiescent consonantal ی, whatever may be the vowels or quiescences of the original word ; as, حَسَن (hàsàn), حُسَيْن (hùsèyn) ; حِصْن (hĭsn), حُصَيْن (hùsàyn) ; &c.

The Persian and Arabic diminutive applies equally to substantives and adjectives. The Arabic rule has many modifications in details. But as these Persian and Arabic diminutives are taken into Ottoman use as original words, enough has been said on their subject for the present purpose.

SECTION II. *The Noun Adjective.*

As a general rule, the adjective, in Turkish, is invariable, having no gender, number, case, or degrees of comparison; and this, whether the word be of Turkish, Arabic, or Persian origin. It always precedes the substantive qualified; as, بیوك آدَم (biyûk âdâm), *a great man,* بیوك آدَملَر (biyûk âdâmlâr), *great men;* بیوك اینَكلَر (biyûk inèklèr), *big cows.*

But the Persian form of phrase is also much used (especially in writing), by which an adjective of Persian or Arabic origin follows the substantive qualified; such adjective remaining in the singular after a Persian substantive plural, the substantive qualified always taking an ésère of subjection to join it to the adjective; thus, مَردَان بُزُرك (mèrdâni bûzûrg), *great men;* عَملْهَای نیك ('âmèlhâyi nîk), *good works.*

If, in this Persian construction, both words are Arabic, and the substantive is a feminine singular, or an irregular plural of any kind, the adjective must be put in the feminine singular, or in an irregular plural form; as, عَسَاكِر مُنتَظِمَه ('âsâkiri mûntâzîmè), *regular troops,* سَلاطِین عِظَام (sèlâtîni 'izâm), *great Sultans.*

Persian adjectives have three degrees of comparison, more or less in use in Turkish composition. The comparative is formed by adding the syllable تَر (tèr) to the end of the positive; and the superlative, by adding the syllables تَرِين (térīn); but these never qualify preceding substantives, being only used as substantive members of phrases, or to qualify a following substantive; thus, بِهْتَرِين وَسَائِل نَجَات (bìhtérìnì vésā-ìlì néjāt), *the best of the means of salvation;* (bìhtérin vésā-ìlì néjāt), *the best means of salvation.*

Arabic adjectives have but two degrees of comparison. Whatever the form of the positive, the comparative is of the form اَفْعَل (éf'ál). This is used, in Persian construction, more as an exaggeration than as a degree of comparison, more as a substantive than an adjective. If followed by a substantive singular, it is a superlative with the sense of *very, extremely, exceedingly,* and the like; thus, اَحْسَن وَسِيلَهِ نَجَات (áhsánì vésīlé-ì néjāt), *a very good means of salvation.* If the following substantive be in the plural, the adjective is a superlative, with the sense of *the most......;* as, اَحْسَن وَسَائِل نَجَات (áhsánì vésā-ìlì néjāt), *the best of the means of salvation.*

If an adjective be used as a substantive, it admits the plural and the prepositions, as substantives; thus, اَيُولَر (ìyúlér), *the good;* اَيُولَرِن (ìyúlérìñ), *of the good,* &c., &c.

Every Turkish adjective, besides its positive signification, betokens, on occasions, the comparative, the superlative, and an excess of the quality it expresses, which we explain by employing the adverb *too* before the word. Thus, بِيُوك (bìyúk), *large, larger, largest, too large;* صِيَاقْ (sìjâq), *hot, hotter, hottest, too hot;* صُوغُرَقْ (sòghùq), *cold, colder, coldest, too cold;* &c.

The Persian compound adjective, much used in Turkish, in the positive degree only, is of many kinds. Some are compounded of two substantives, one or both of which may be Arabic or Persian, never Turkish; as, جَمْ جَنَابْ (jèm-jènāb), *majestic as Jemshīd;* آصَفْ تَدْبِيرْ (āsâf-tèdbīr), *Asaph in counsel;* شَكَرْلَبْ (shèkèr-lèb), *sugar-lipped;* عَدَالَتْ دَسْتْكَاهْ ('âdālèt-dèstgyâh), *a very loom of justice* (i. e., *just*); others of an adjective followed by a substantive; as, سَبُكْپَاى (sèbûk-pāy), *light of foot, light-footed;* or a substantive followed by an adjective; as, دِلْ تِشْنَ (dìl-tìshnè), *thirsty-hearted* (i. e., *ardently desirous*); or a substantive preceded by هَمْ (hèm); as, هَمْ آشْيَانَ (hèm-āshyānè), *of the same nest;* هَمْجِنْسْ (hèm-jìns), *of the same genus;* هَمْشَهْرِى (hèm-shèhrī), *of the same town or country, a fellow-countryman;* of a substantive followed by وَشْ (vèsh), *like;* as, پَرِى وَشْ (pèrī-vèsh), *fairy-like;* of a substantive followed by رَنْك (rȧng), فَمْ (fām), or گُونْ (gyūn), all signifying *colour;* as, سَبْزرَنْك (sèbz-rȧng), *green-coloured;* زُمُردْفَامْ (zùmûrrùd-fām), *emerald-coloured;* گَنْدُمْ گُونْ (gèndûm-gyūn), *wheat-coloured* (i. e., *dark-complexioned, brown*); of a substantive followed by شِيرِينْ كَارْ (kyār, gyār), گَرْ (gèr), بَانْ (bān), or دَارْ (dār); as, شِيرِينْ كَارْ (shīrīn-kyār), *sweet-mannered;* آفَرِيدْ كَارْ (āfèrìd-gyār), *creative*

(i. e., *creator*) ; زَرْگَر (zèr-gèr), *goldworker, goldsmith* ; بَاغْبَان
(bāg-bān), *garden-keeper* (i. e., *gardener*) ; مُهْرْدَار (mûhr-dār), *seal-
keeper* ; or followed by دَان (dān), زَار (zār), سَار (sār), or اسْتَان
(istàn), *all names of special places* ; as, قَلَمْدَان (qàlèm-dān), *a
pen-case* ; گُلْـزَار (gyûl-zār), *a flower-garden, a flowery mead* ;
كُوهْسَار (kyūh-sār), *mountainous district* ; عَرَبِسْتَان ('àràbistàn),
Arabia; or a substantive repeated ; as, چَاکْچَاک (chàk-chàk),
imitative of the sound of repeated blows with axe or sword ;
the same, or two different substantives, with ا placed between
them ; as, چَاکَاچَاک (chākyā-chāk), same signification, سَرَاپَا (sèr-
ā-pā), *from head to foot;* or with تَا or تَ in place of the ا; as,
سَرْتَاپَا (sèr-tā-pā), *same sense;* سَرْتَسَر (sèr-tè-sèr), *from end to end,
from beginning to end;* or with اَن in شَبَانْرُوز (shèbān-rūz), *night
and day* (which is unique), شَبَانَه رُوز (shèbānè-rūz), *meaning:
a whole night and day, all night and all day, twenty-four hours,
or several nights and days in one succession;* or with some
other Persian preposition between the two ; as, پَيْدَرْپَی pèy-dèr-
pèy), *step by step, gradatim;* دَسْتْ بَرْ دَسْتْ (dèst-bèr-dèst), *hand
on hand, hands crossed;* سِينَه بَسِينَه (sīnè-bè-sīnè), *breast to breast;*
دُوشَادُوش (dūsh-à-dūsh), *shoulder to shoulder, back to back;* سَرْبَمُهْر
(sèr-bè-mûhr), *with the head* (or mouth of a bag, bottle, &c.)
sealed up; or with a substantive and compound adjective ; as,
بَخْتْ بَرْگَشْتَه (bàkht-bèr-gèshtè), *whose luck is reversed;* or even

four words combined; as, سَرْبَفَلَكْ كَشِيدَه (sèr-bè-fèlèk-kèshīdè), *whose head is lifted up to the very spheres;* besides many other varieties; especially the two privatives in بی (bī), *without,* and نَا (nā), *not;* as, بی اَدَبْ (bī-èdèb), *without education* or *manners, unmannerly, impolite;* نَابِينَا (nā-bīnā), *not seeing, sightless, blind.*

Some Arabic expressions may be regarded as compound epithets in Turkish and Persian; as, صَاحِبْقِرَانْ (sāhíb-qĭrān), *lord of the conjunction* (i. e., *the master of the age*); وَلِیِ نِعْمَتْ (vèlī-nǐ'mèt), *associate of benefits* (i. e., *a benefactor*); expressions formed of ذُو (zū), ذَاتْ (zāt), اَهْلْ (èhl), and اَرْبَابْ (èrbāb), all of which imply *possession;* as, ذُو ذُوَابَه (zū-zǔ᾽ābè), *possessed of a forelock or topknot,* and ذُو ذُنَابَه (zū-zǔnābè), *possessed of a following* (i.e., *a comet*); ذَاتُ الْجَنْبْ (zātǔ-'l-jènb, *vulg.* sàtlǐjāu), *the possessor of the side* (i. e., *pleurisy*); or in Persian construction; as, اَهْلِ عِرْضْ (èhlǐ-'ĭrz), *possessed of honour or virtue, honorable, honest, virtuous;* اَرْبَابْ مَسْنَدْ (èrbābǐ-mèsnèd), *those who possess the chief seat* (i. e., *high dignitaries*); or an adjective qualified with غَیْر (gàyr), *other;* as, غَیْرِ مَحْدُودْ (gàyrǐ-màhdūd), *other than circumscribed* (i. e., *unlimited, undefined*); or an Arabic verb in the aorist made negative with لَا (lā), *not;* as, لَا یُحْصَا (lā-yǔhsà), *not to be counted, innumerable;* لَا یُعَدّ (lā-yǔ'àdd), *untold, innumerable;* لَا یَمُوتْ (lā-yèmūt), *who dies not, immortal;* لَا یَتَجَزَّا (lā-yètèjèzzà), *not to be subdivided, indivisible;* or an

Arabic adjective followed by a definite article and substantive;
as, اَبَدِىُّ ٱلدَّوَام (èbèdìyyù-'d-dèvām), *eternal in duration*; قَوِىُّ ٱلْبُنْيَان
(qàvìyyù-'l-bùnyān), *strong in build;* &c., &c., &c.

Every Turkish adjective is also an adverb; that is to say,
that, without any modification of form, the Turkish adjective
qualifies verbs as well as substantives; thus, كُوزَلْ آتْ (gyùzèl àt),
a beautiful stallion; كُوزَلْ يُورُيمَكْ (gyùzèl yùrùmèk), *to walk
gracefully.* The same is the case with Persian adjectives,
whether used in Turkish or in Persian phrases. Arabic
adjectives, as Arabic substantives, require to be put in their
own accusative case indefinite when used as adverbs; as, فِعْلًا
(fì'làn), *by act;* حَسَنًا (hàsànàn), *beautifully.* Arabic substantives are also sometimes used as Turkish adverbs by being put
in their own genitive, indefinite or definite, as may be, and
preceded by an Arabic preposition; as, عَنْ غَفْلَة ('àn gàflètìn),
by inadvertence; عَلَى ٱلتَّوَالِى ('àlè-'t-tèvàlì), *in continued succession, successively;* فِى ٱلْحَقِيقَه (fì-'l-hàqìqà), *in reality, really,
truly;* بِٱلدَّفَعَات (bì-'d-dèfà'àt), *on several occasions, repeatedly;*
لِسَبَب (lì-sèbèbìn), *for a reason;* &c.

As with substantives, so also every Turkish adjective has
its diminutive, formed by the addition of the suffix جَه (jè, jà),
-ish, to the word, whether this end in a consonant or vowel;
as, يَشِلْ (yèshìl), *green,* يَشِلْجَه (yèshìljè), *greenish, somewhat
green;* قِزِلْ (qìzìl) *red,* قِزِلْجَه (qìzìljà) *reddish;* بِيُوكْ (bìyùk)

large, بِيُوكْجَه (blyûkjè) *largish;* أُوفَاق (ûfâq) *small,* أُوفَاجَه
(ûfâqjâ) *smallish;* ايرى (Irí) *large,* ايرِيجَه (Irljè) *largish;* قَرَه
(qârâ) *black,* قَرَهجَه (qârâjâ) *blackish;* قُورُو (qûrû) *dry,* قُورُوجَه
(qûrûjâ) *dryish.* A modification of this form, dictated by the
principle of euphony, is used for the words بِيُوكْ, كِجُوكْ, أُوفَاق,
by substituting a final كْ or ڭ for the ه, and suppressing those
letters at the end of the radical word, as for substantives; thus,
بِيُوجَكْ (blyûjèk), *largish.* A further conformity with the sense
of euphony, avoiding two أُوسْتُنْ vowels in succession, makes
أُوفَاجِق (ûfâjîq) *smallish,* and كِجُوجَكْ (kûchûjûk) *smallish;* this
last being doubly euphonic.

These diminutive adjectives, as in every language, often
express in Turkish the reverse of diminution in the quality
they represent, being in fact exaggeratives in sense, and meaning *very, exceedingly, extremely,* &c.; as, جَسُورْجَه آدَمْ دِرْ (jèsûrjâ
âdâm dîr), *he is a bravish man* (i. e., *a very brave man*).

Section III. *The Numerals.*

Turkish, Arabic, and Persian numerals, cardinal and ordinal,
are used in Ottoman. Arabic fractions are also used as far as
one-tenth. In this sketch, however, the five sorts of Turkish
numerals alone are explained. These are the cardinal, ordinal,
distributive, fractional, and indefinite numbers.

The simple Turkish cardinal numbers are : بِرْ (bĭr) *one,*
اِیکِی (ĭkĭ) *two,* اُوچْ (ûch) *three,* دُرْت (dûrt) *four,* بَشْ (bêsh) *five,*
آلْتِی (âltĭ) *six,* یَدِی (yêdĭ) *seven,* سَكِزْ (sêkĭz) *eight,* طُقُوزْ (dôqûz)
nine, اُونْ (ôn) *ten,* یِکِرْمِی (yĭyĭrmĭ) *twenty,* اُوتُوزْ (ôtûz), *thirty,*
قِرْق (qĭrq) *forty,* اَلْلِی (êllĭ) *fifty,* اَلْتْمِشْ (âltmĭsh) *sixty,* یَتْمِشْ (yêt-
mĭsh) *seventy,* سَكْسَانْ (sêksân) *eighty,* طُقْسَانْ (dôqsân) *ninety,*
یُوزْ (yûz) *a hundred,* بِیكْ (bĭñ) *a thousand.* The two substantives, یُوكْ (yûk), *a hundred thousand,* and مِلْیُونْ (mĭlyôn), *a*
million, are also used; but they are not true numerals. They
are names of aggregates, and require the numerals before
them; as, بِرْ یُوكْ (bĭr yûk), *one hundred thousand,* بِرْ مِلْیُونْ (bĭr
mĭlyôn) *one million;* and so on for higher numbers, اِیکِی یُوكْ,
اُونْ مِلْیُونْ, &c. The French numerals بِلْیُونْ (bĭlyôn), تِرِلْیُونْ (tĭrĭl-
yôn), &c., are sometimes used.

The compound Turkish cardinal numerals are uniformly
built up by putting the units after the tens up to 99, and by
placing the word یُوزْ before the simple or compound expression
up to 199; then by adding the units from 2 to 9 before یُوزْ
up to 999; next by using بِیكْ before these simples or compounds up to 1999; and finally, by again using the simples
or compounds before بِیكْ up to 999,999; thus, اُونْبِرْ (ôn-bĭr)
eleven, یِکِرْمِی اِیکِی (yĭyĭrmĭ ĭkĭ) *twenty-two,* یُوزْ اُوتُوزْ اُوچْ (yûz ôtûz
ûch) *one hundred and thirty-three,* بِیكْ سَكِزْ یُوزْ قِرْق بَشْ (bĭñ

séklz yůz qírq bésh) *one thousand eight hundred and forty-five,*

بَش يُوزْ اَلْتَمِشْ سَكِزْ بِيكْ يُوزْ اُونْدُرْتْ (bésh yůz åltmísh séklz blñ yůz

ôn důrt) 568,114, اُوچ مِلْيُونْ يِدِى يُوكْ طُقْسَان اِيكِى بِيكْ اُوچْيُوزْ اَلْلِى اَلْتِى

(ůch mílyôn, yédl yůk, dåqsån lkl blñ, ůch yůz, élll åltí)

3,792,356. It will be noticed that no conjunction enters these
combinations. When the foreign expression مِلْيُونْ, or the
treasury word يُوكْ is not used, the native method of expressing
multiples of يُوزْبِيكْ is to state the simple or compound
number of such multiple, and then to intercalate the word

كَرَّه (kérré) *times*, before the word يُوزْبِيكْ; as, يِدِى كَرَّه يُوزْبِيكْ

(yédl kérré yůz blñ) *seven times one hundred thousand,* 700,000 ;

دُرْتْ يُوزْ اَلْلِى اِيكِى كَرَّه يُوزْبِيكْ (důrt yůz élll lkl kérré yůz blñ)
45,200,000.

The Turkish interrogative cardinal numeral is قَاچْ (qåch)
how many?

The cardinal numerals are adjectives; but, like all adjectives, may be used as substantives, and declined. Even the
interrogative قَاچْ is used as a substantive when enquiring
"*what number?*" or "*what is it o'clock?*" or "*at what price?*"
or "*what is the day of the month?*" Thus: قَاچْ دِيدِيكِزْ (qåch
dldlñlz) "*how many did you say?*" سَاعَتْ قَاچَه كَلْدِى (sūåt qåchå
gåldl) "*to how many (hours) has the clock come?*" قَاچَه وِيرِيُورْسِينْ
(qåchå vérlyôrsůn) "*at how much art thou selling (it, them)?*"

در قاچی آیك (āylñ qáchî dlr) "*the how-manyeth of the month is it?*"

The Persian compound cardinals place the higher elements first, as in Turkish and English; but the conjunction و is introduced between each two members; as, هَزَار و دُوِيسْت و شَصْت و هَفْت (hèzār ů dåwist ů shåst ů hèft), *a thousand, two hundred, and sixty-seven.*

The Arabic compound cardinals take the conjunction و between each pair also; but the lower elements stand first; as, سَنَه تِسْعُ وخَمْسِينُ و مِأَتَيْنِ وأَلْفٌ (sèné-i tis' ů khåmsīn ů mľètèyn ů èlf) *the year one thousand two hundred and fifty-nine,* expressed in Turkish, بِيكْ اِيـكِـيُـوزْ أَللِى طُقُوزْ سَنَسِى (blñ ĭklyůz èllî dòqůz sènèsl).

The Turkish ordinal numbers are formed by adding an èsèrè to the last quiescent consonant of the cardinal, simple or compound, followed by the termination نْجى; as, بِرِنْجى (blrlnjl) *first,* اُوتُوزْنْجى (òtůzůnjů) *thirtieth,* يُوزْنْجى (yůzůnjů) *hundredth,* بِيكْنْجى (blñlnjl) *thousandth,* بِيكْ بَشْيُوزْ قِرْق طُقُوزْنْجى ,الَّلِى سَكِزِنْجى But, in the numbers that end in vowel ى, this is suppressed before the same termination; as, اِيكِنْجى (ĭklnjl) *second,* أَلْتِنْجى (åltlnjl) *sixth,* يَدِنْجى (yèdlnjl) *seventh,* يِـكِـرْمِنْجى (ylyĭrmlnjl) *twentieth,* اَللِنْجى (èllĭnjl) *fiftieth.* The cardinal دُرْت changes its final into د before the ordinal termination; as, اُونْ دَرْدُنْجى (òn-dårdůnjů) *fourteenth.*

The Arabic and Persian ordinals are frequently used, and may be found in the lexicons, &c.

The Turkish distributive numbers are formed from the cardinals by making their last quiescent consonant movent with üstün, and then adding a quiescent ر to the word; as, بِرَر (bírér), بَشَر (béshér), اُوتُوزَر (ótúzér); يُوزَر (yúzér), بِيكَر (bíñér). Their sense is expressed in English, which has no such numerals, by the words *each* and *apiece;* the foregoing examples will thus be rendered : *one each, five apiece, thirty each, a hundred each, a thousand each.* The cardinal دُرْت becomes دُرْدَر (dúrdér) *four apiece.*

When the cardinal ends with a vowel, the syllable شَر (shér) is suffixed to form the distributive ; as, اِيكِشَر (íkíshér) *two apiece,* اَلْتِيشَر (áltíshér) *six each,* يَدِيشَر (yédíshér) *seven apiece,* بِكْرِمِيشَر (yíyírmíshér) *twenty each,* اَلْلِيشَر (éllíshér) *fifty each.*

In the case of more than one hundred or thousand, it is the cardinal that designates their number that receives the distributive suffix ; as, اِيكِشَر يُوز (íkíshér yúz) *two hundred each,* بَشَر بِيڭ (béshér bíñ) *five thousand apiece.* And in compound numbers the distributive suffixes are added to the numbers of thousands, of hundreds, and of final units or tens, to indicate one distribution ; thus, بَشَر يُوز بِكْرِمِی بِرَر (béshér yúz yíyírmí bírér) *five hundred and twenty-one each,* سَكِزَر بِيڭ يَدِيشَر يُوز قِرْق اِيكِشَر (sékízér bíñ, yédíshér yúz, qîrq íkíshér), 8,742 *apiece ;* يُوز اَلْلِيشَر (yúz éllíshér), 150 *each.*

The Turkish fractional numbers are very simple. The number of the denominator in the locative, and followed by the number of the numerator is the form; as, اِيكِيدَه بِرْ (ikidè bir) *in two* (parts), *one; i.e.* ½, *the half;* بَشْدَه اِيكِى (beshdè iki) *in five, two; i.e.* ⅖, *two-fifths.* Sometimes one of the synonyms پاى (pāy), جُزْ (jûz'), قِسْم (qism), حِصَّه (hissà) *part,* is added after each numeral of the fraction; as, اِيكِى پَايْدَه بِرْ پَاى (iki pāydà, bir pāy) *in two parts, one part.*

The Arabic fractional numbers are also used up to ten. Excepting the word نِصْف (nisf) *a half, the half,* they are all of the form فُعْل; thus, ثُلْث (sûls, *vulg.* sûlûs) *a third,* رُبْع (rûb') *a fourth,* خُمْس (khûms) *a fifth,* سُدْس (sûds) *a sixth,* سُبْع (sûb') *a seventh,* ثُمْن (sûmn) *an eighth,* تُسْع (tûs') *a ninth,* عُشْر ('ushr, *vulg.* 'ushûr) *a tenth, a tithe.* The dual of ثُلْث is used, ثُلْثَان (sûlsān) *two-thirds;* but for all the others a Turkish numerator is used; as, أُوچْ رُبْع (ûch rûb') *three quarters,* اِيكِى خُمْس (iki khûms) *two-fifths,* بَشْ تُسْع (besh tûs') *five-ninths,* &c.

There are two special Turkish adjectives and one Turkish substantive to express *half.* One of the adjectives, يَارِم (yàrim), and the substantive, يَارِى (yàri), signify *the half* (of one sole thing; as, يَارِم أَلْمَا (yàrim èlmà) *half an apple, a half apple;* أَلْمَانِڭ يَارِيسِى (èlmànin yàrisi), *the half of an* (or *of the*) *apple.* The other adjective, بُوچُوقْ (bûchûq), is used after some whole number, never alone ; as, بِرْ بُوچُوقْ اَلْمَا (bĭr bŭchŭq ĕlmă) *an apple and a half,* ایكی بُوچُوقْ سَاعَتْ (ĭkĭ bŭchŭq sā'ăt) *two hours and a half.*

When a complex fractional number consisting of an integer and a fraction other than *one-half* has to be expressed, the Turkish or Arabic fractions are used, the conjunction وَ or the preposition ایلَه being introduced between the integer and the fraction ; as, اِیكِی ایلَه بِرْ رُبْعْ or اِیكِی وَ بِرْ رُبْعْ *two and one-fourth.* When the Turkish fraction is used, the numeral بِرْ in the genitive is also introduced before the fraction ; as, بَشْ ایلَه بِرِكْ سَكِزْدَه اُوچِی *five, and three-eighths of one.*

The indefinite numerals are : هَرْ (hĕr) *every ;* هَرْ بِرْ (hĕr bĭr) *every one, each ;* هیچْ (hĭch) *no, none ;* هیچْ بِرْ (hĭch bĭr), *no ;* بَعْضِ (bă'zĭ) *some ;* اَكْثَرْ (ĕksĕr) *the most part ;* بِرْ قَاچْ (bĭr qăch) *some, a few ;* آزْ (ăz) *few ;* چُوقْ (chŏq) *many ;* بِرْ آزْ (bĭr ăz) *a few, a little ;* بِرْ چُوقْ (bĭr chŏq) *a great many, a great quantity ;* &c. Of these, هَرْ is always an adjective; the rest are adjectives and substantives.

There is a small series of Turkish numerals of a peculiar nature, from ایكیز (ĭkĭz), *twin, twins,* through اُوچُوز (ŭchŭz) *triple, a trine,* دُردُیز (dŭrdŭz) *fourfold,* to بَشیز (bĕshĭz) *five-fold,* and perhaps on to اُونُیز (ŏnŭz) *ten-fold.* Adjectives are formed

from these in لُو ; as, ايكيزلُو (ikizlĭ), *possessed of twins, of twin*
(branches, &c.) ; اُوچُيزلُو (ûchûzlû) *with three* (lambs, branches,
&c.) ; &c.

The written digits are : ۱ 1, ۲ 2, ۳ 3, ۴ 4, ۵ 5, ۶ 6, ۷ 7, ۸ 8,
۹ 9, ۰ 0. With these, compound numbers are written as in
English, from left to right ; as, ۲۵ 25, ۱۶۰ 160, ۳۴۰۹ 3409,
۷۸۰۰۳۰۴۶ 78003046, &c.

In dates, the thousand, and generally the hundreds, of the
year of the Hijra are omitted, as also the dots of the letters ;
thus, سنـه stands for سنـه۱۲۹۶ (sèné biñ ikiyûz dôqsán áltí)
in the year (of the Hijra) 1296 ; سنـه دا ۲۱ ى (fī yiyirmi bir
zā, sèné 97) *on the 21st Zī-'l-Qa'da, '97* (A.H.).

The signs for the months, in dates, are : م, for مُحَرَّم ; ص, for
صَفَر ; را, forرَبِيعُ ٱلاَوَّل ; ر, for رَبِيعُ ٱلآخِرْ ; حا, for جَمَاذى ٱلاَوَّل ;
ح, for جَمَاذى ٱلآخِرْ ; ب, for رَجَبْ ; س, for شَعْبَان ; ن, for رَمَضَان ;
ل, for شَوَّالْ ; دا, for ذِى ٱلْقَعْدَه ; د, for ذِى ٱلْحَجَّ. The day
always precedes the sign of the month ; and the first day is
termed غُرِّه (gùrré), while the thirtieth is named سَلْخْ (sèlkh) ;
as, ۲۵ م عرا ى, وى ص سله م سله ; all dots being omitted in
these shortened numeral dates. Not so, however, when the
date is written out in full words ; as, اِشْبُو بِيڭ اِيكِيوُز طُقْسَان
كُونِى پَنْجْشَنْبِه بَشِنْجِى اُون مُحَرَّمِنڭ مَاهِ هِجْرِيَّهسى سَنَهء طُقُوز) (ishbù biñ
ikiyûz dôqsán dôquz sèné'l hijriyyési māh-i mûbárréminiñ ôn

béshInjl pénjshénbih gyûnd) *This day of Thursday, the 15th of
the month of Muharrem, of the Hijra year* 1299.

<h2 style="text-align:center">SECTION IV. The Pronoun.</h2>

The Turkish personal pronoun has no distinction of gender:
بَن (bén) *I*, سَن (sân, *not* sén) *thou*, اُو (ó; in writing, generally,
اُول ól) *he, she, it ;* and their plurals : بِز (blz) *we*, سِز (slz) *you,*
اَنْلَر (ânlâr, ónlâr) *they.*

In politeness, بِز and سِـز are used instead of بَن and سَن.
They then have their own plurals: بِزْلَر (blzlér), سِزْلَر (slzlér),
which cannot be expressed in English. These are even used
as singulars, by the over-polite. The third person plural is
used, in the same way, out of politeness, for the singular, as
is practised in Italian ; but it has not its plural. The word
كَنْدِى (kéndl) *self,* is a kind of common pronoun, of all the
persons, singular and plural. It is specialized by the possessives.

The personal pronouns, singular and plural, are declined in
the same way as the nouns substantive, excepting that some of
them have a special genitive,—all but those of the second
person, singular and plural. These genitives are: بَنِم (bénlm)
of me, my ; سَنِك (sânlñ) *of thee, thy ;* اَنِك (ânlñ, ónlñ) *of him,
her, it ; his, her, its ;* بِزِم (blzlm) *of us, our;* سِزِك (slzlñ) *of you,
your ;* اَنْلَرِك (ânlârlñ, ónlârlñ) *of them, their.* But, to take either

of the prepositions اِيجُوْن , اِيلَه , after their singulars, they must
be put in the genitive, all but the third person plural; as,
آنْـكَرِ ايلَه for me, سِرْكَ ايلَه with you, آنڭ اِيجُوْن for him, her, it, بِنِم اِيجُوْن
with them.

These genitives are used, *when required*, to emphasize and
corroborate the possessive pronoun of the same number and
person. They are never used alone, without their possessives
to corroborate; thus, بَابَام (bâbâm) my *father* (not my *mother*,
&c.), بَنِم بَابَام (bénim bâbâm) *my* father (not *your* father, or *his*
father).

The possessive pronouns, too, have no distinction of gender,
either on the English or French principle. They are مْ (im,
îm) *my*; كْ (iñ, îñ) *thy*; ى (i, î), or, after a vowel, سى (si, sî)
his, her, its; مِزْ (imiz, îmîz) *our*, كِزْ (iñiz, îñîz) *your*; لَرِى (lèri,
lârî), *their*.

These possessives are suffixed to the substantives they
qualify, and form one word with them. That compound
word is then declined like a simple substantive; thus, أَوِيم
(évim) *my house*, أَوِيمِڭ (évimiñ) *of my house*, أَوِيمَه (évimé) *to
my house*, أَوِيمْدَه (évimdé) *in my house*; &c. (The ى added
here before the bare possessive, is thought by some to be
needed in the case of a preceding consonant that does not
join on in writing to its next letter in the same word. Others
do not consider it necessary, and write: أَوِم, أَوِڭ, أَوِى, &c.; but

when the compound, in declension, &c., takes another vowel
after it, it is more usual to add this preceding vowel also; as,
اوِيكِنْ (èvìmìñ) *of my house,* اوِيمَه (èvìmè) *to my house;*
(èvìñìz) *your house; &c.*

The vowel that precedes the bare possessive is an èsèrè, soft
or hard, given grammatically to the final consonant of the
qualified substantive, when it ends in a consonant. Thus,
آتْ (àt) *a horse,* آتِمْ (àtìm) *my horse,* آتِكْ (àtìñ) *thy horse,*
(àtì), *his, her, its horse,* آتِمِزْ (àtìmìz) *our horse,* آتِكِزْ (àtìñìz)
your horse, آتلَرِي (àtlàrì) *their horse.* After an ùtùrù vowel
dominant, this èsèrè becomes ùtùrù also; thus, اوغُلْ (òghùl)
a son, اوغُلُمْ (òghùlùm) *my son;* بُوتْ (bùt) *a thigh,* بُوتُمْ (bùtùm)
or بُودُمْ (bùdùm) *my thigh;* يُوزْ (yùz) *a face,* يُوزُمْ (yùzùm) *my
face;* كُوزْ (gyùz) *an eye,* كُوزُمْ (gyùzùm) *my eye.*

When the substantive ends with a vowel, the bare possessive
is added to form a syllable with that vowel, whatever it may
be; thus, بَابَامْ (bàbàm) *my father;* يَانْقُوكْ (yànqòñ) *thy echo;*
قَپُوسِي (qàpùsù) *his, her, its door or gate;* سُونْكُومُزْ (sùngyùmùz)
our bayonet; كُورْكُوكُزْ (gyùrgyùñùz) *your experience;* سُورُولَرِي
(sùrùlèrì) *their flock.* The example here given, with the
possessive singular of the third person, shows clearly that
when the substantive ends with a vowel, سِى is the possessive,
in lieu of ى after a consonant.

If the final vowel of the substantive is ه, it is never joined

on to the possessive in writing. Thus, تَيْزَمْ (téyzém) *my*
(maternal) *aunt,* تَيْزَنْ (téyzéñ), *thy aunt,* تَيْزَسِى (téyzési) *his or*
her aunt; تَيْزَمِز (téyzémlz) *our aunt,* تَيْزَكِز (téyzéñlz) *your aunt,*
تَيْزَلَرِى (téyzéléri) *their aunt.*

When the final vowel is ى, the possessives of the first and
second persons singular do not join on to it in writing. In
the third person singular, and in all the possessive plurals,
they join on. Thus, تَرْزِى (térzl) *a tailor,* تَرْزِيمْ (térzlm) *my*
tailor, تَرْزِيكْ (térzlñ) *thy tailor,* تَرْزِيسِى (térzlsl) *his or her tailor,*
تَرْزِيمِز (térzlmlz) *our tailor,* تَرْزِيكِز (térzlñlz) *your tailor,* تَرْزِيلَرِى
(térzlléri) *their tailor.* There is no valid reason for this rule;
custom alone has it so. Thus are formed: كَنْدِمْ (kéndlm)
myself, كَنْدِنْ (kéndlñ) *thyself,* كَنْدِيسِى (kéndlsl) *his, her, itself;*
كَنْدِيمِز (kéndlmlz) *ourselves,* كَنْدِيكِز (kéndlñlz) *yourselves,* كَنْدِيلَرِى
(kéndlléri) *theirselves.*

A final ق, in a polysyllable, as in declension, changes into
غ before the possessives, singular or plural, excepting that of
the third person plural; so also, an Arabic ك changes into
Turkish ك (*y* value) in like cases. Thus, قُونَاق (qónáq), *a*
mansion, قُونَاغِمْ (qónághlm) *my mansion;* ايپَكْ (lpék) *silk,*
ايپَكْ (lpéylñ) *thy silk;* طَاوُق (táwúq) *a fowl,* طَاوُغُى (táwúghú)
his or her fowl; قُونَاغِمِز (qónághlmlz) *our mansion,*
(lpéylñlz) *your silk;* طَاوُقلَرِى (táwúqlári) *their fowl.* The

reason of the exception is evident,—the final consonant takes no vowel before لَرِى.

These possessives equally qualify plural substantives, and follow the sign of the plural. Thus, أَوْلَرِمْ (évlérìm), *my houses;* اتـلَـرِك (àtlàrìñ) *thy horses;* سُونْكُوْلَرِى (süngyûléri) *his, her, its bayonets;* سُورُولَرِيمِز (sûrûlérìmìz) *our flocks;* تَيْزَوْلَرِيكِزْ (téyzéléri-ñìz) *your aunts;* قُونَاقْلَرِى (qònàqlàrì) *their mansions.*

By a consideration of the examples above given with the possessives of the third persons, singular and plural, as attached to singular and plural substantives, two peculiarities become evident, namely: 1, the plural sign is not repeated for the possessive when the substantive is itself plural; 2, consequently, the combination of a substantive and a possessive of the third person, when it has the plural syllable لَرْ between the two, leaves it altogether doubtful whether this plural sign belongs to the substantive or to the possessive. Even if the combination قُونَاقْلَرِلَرِى (qònàqlàrléri) had been in use,—which is not the case,—it would have been impossible to decide whether قُونَاقْلَرِى (qònàqlàrì) was intended to betoken the sense of *his* or *her mansions,* on the one hand, or *their mansion,* on the other. Add to this difficulty the third sense of *their mansions,* and the puzzle becomes still more complicated. In conversation, the doubt of the hearer may be removed, if necessary, by proper enquiries. But, in a written document, intended to be understood by an absent reader, possibly after the death of the writer, a method was seen, especially by judges and legists, to be necessary for distinguishing between the three cases.

That distinction is effected, in writing, somewhat at the expense of plain grammar, as follows. To distinguish the single possessor of the plural possessions, the singular corroborative genitive of the personal pronoun is placed before the combination containing the plural sign; thus, اَنِكَ قُوۡنَاقۡلَرِی (ánìñ qònàqlàrì) *his* or *her* mansions. To distinguish the plural joint possessors of a single possession, the genitive of the plural personal pronoun is prefixed, and grammar is violated by omitting the plural sign from the combination of substantive and possessive; as, اَنۡلَرِكۡ قُوۡنَغِی (ánlàrìñ qònàghì) *their mansion*. In the third case, the sign of the plural is used in the corroborative and in the combination; thus, اَنۡلَرِكۡ قُوۡنَاقۡلَرِی (ánlàrìñ qònàqlàrì) *their mansions*. A doubt may still be felt, and these distinctions are not always used.

The declension of the combination with the possessive of the third person, singular or plural, takes a special form, a ن being introduced before the prepositions, and the final vowel-letter of the original combination suppressed before this ن, when the latter is joined in writing to the combination singular, or does not itself possess a vowel in the combination plural. This rule, applied to possessives joined to substantives ending respectively in consonants or vowels, acts thus:

كِتَابْلَرِيثك ; كِتَابِنْدَنْ , كِتَابِنِى , كِتَابِنْدَه , كِتَابِنَه , كِتَابِثك , كِتَابِى

تَيْزَهسِنَه , تَيْزَهسِنْك , تَيْزَهسِى ; كِتَابْلَرِنْدَنْ , كِتَابْلَرِينِى , كِتَابْلَرِنْدَه , كِتَابْلَرِينَه

تَيْزَهلَرِنْدَه , تَيْزَهلَرِينَه , تَيْزَهلَرِثك , تَيْزَهلَرِى ; تَيْزَهسِنْدَنْ , تَيْزَهسِنِى , تَيْزَهسِنْدَه

تَيْزَهلَرِنْدَنْ , تَيْزَهلَرِينِى .

When كَنْدِى is an adjective, it remains unchanged, and means *own*; thus, كَنْدِى بَابَامْ (kêndî bâbâm) *my own father*, كَنْدِى وَالِدَهلَرِيكِزْ (kêndî vâlîdêlêrîñîz) *your own mothers*, &c.

SECTION V. *The Demonstratives.*

These are, بُو (bû) *this*, شُو (shû) *that or this*, أُو (ô) or أُوّل (ôl, as in the personal) *that*, أُوبِرْ (ô-bîr) or أُولْبِرْ (ôl-bîr) *the other*. They are used as substantives and as adjectives; being declined or invariable, accordingly, like other substantives and adjectives. Thus, بُو كِتَابْ *this book*, بُو كِتَابْلَرْ *these books*; أُوبِرْ أَدَمْ *that other man*, أُوبِرْ آدَمْ *those other men*; &c.

As substantives, بُو and شُو are thus declined, something like the personal أُو or أُوّل: بُو (bû), بُونُك (bûnûñ), بُوكَا (bûñâ), بُونْدَه (bûndâ), بُونْدَنْ (bûndân); بُونْلَرْ (bûnlâr), بُونْلَرِك (bûnlârîñ), بُونِى (bûnû), بُونْدَنْ (bûndân); بُونْلَرْ (bûnlâr), بُونْلَرِك (bûnlârîñ), بُونْلَرَه (bûnlârâ), بُونْلَرْدَه (bûnlârdâ), بُونْلَرِى (bûnlârî),

بُونْلَرْدَنْ (bûnlârdân) ; شُو (shû, sometimes written شُوْل, pronounced shôl), شُونُكْ (shûnûñ), شُوكَا (shûñâ), شُونْدَه (shûndâ),
شُونُى (shûnû), شُونْدَنْ (shûndân) ; شُونْلَرْ (shûnlâr), شُونْلَرَكْ (shûn-
lârîñ), شُونْلَرَه (shûnlârâ) ; شُونْلَرْدَه (shûnlârdâ), شُونْلَرِى (shûnlârî),
شُونْلَرْدَنْ (shûnlârdân). With ايچُون and ايلَه their singulars are
put in the genitive; as, بُونُكْ ايچُون *for this,* شُونُكْ ايلَه *with that.*

But اُوبِرْ, to be used as a substantive, must have the possessive suffix of the third person appended to it; اُوبِرِى (ô-blrl)
its other one, the other one (of the two). It is then declined
like all similar combinations : اُوبِرِينِى, اُوبِرِنْدَه, اُوبِرِينَه, اُوبِرِينِكْ,
اُوبِرْلَرْنْدَنْ, اُوبِرْلَرِينِى, اُوبِرْلَرِنْدَه, اُوبِرْلَرِينَه, اُوبِرْلَرِينِكْ, اُوبِرْلَرِى ; اُوبِرِنْدَنْ.
Or it may take either of the two possessive suffixes of the first
and second persons plural; as, اُوبِرِيمِزْ (ô-blrlmlz), *the other one
of us,* اُوبِرِيمِزْكْ *of the other one of us;* اُوبِرِيكِزَه *to the other one of
you;* اُوبِرْلَرِيمِزْدَه *in the other ones of us;* اُوبِرْلَرِيكِزِى *the other ones
of you;* &c.

SECTION VI. *The Interrogatives.*

كِيمْ (klm) *who?* is always a substantive, and declined as
such, singular and plural: كِيمُكْ *of whom? whose?* كِيمَه *to whom?*
كِيمْدَه *in whom?* كِيمِى *whom?* كِيمْدَنْ *of* or *from whom?* كِيمْلَرْ
who, what or *which persons?* &c.

نَه (nè) *what ?* is generally a substantive, and declined; but it is also used as an adjective, and is then invariable : نَدِنك (nènīñ) *of what ?* نَیَه (for نَدِیَه, nèyè) *to what ?* نَدَه (nèdè) *in what ?* نَدِی (nèyì) *what* (accus.) ? نَدَنْ (for نَدَدَنْ, nèdàn) *from what ?* نَلَر (for نَدَلَرْ, nèlèr) *what* (things)? نَلَرِڭ (nèlèrìñ) *of what* (things); &c.

قَنْغِی (qàngì, *vulg.* hàngì) *which ?* is both substantive and adjective,—declined or invariable accordingly.

These three words, as substantives, take the possessive suffixes. Thus, كِیِمْ (kìmìm) *my who ?* نَـمْ (nèm) *my what ?* كِیِمِڭ (kìmìñ) *thy who ?* نَڭ (nèñ) *thy what ?* قَنْغِیسِی (qàngìsì) *its which, which* (one) *of it ?* كِیِمْلَرِمْ (kìmlèrìm) *my what persons ?* نَلَرِمْ (nèlèrìm) *my what things ?* قَنْغِیمِیزْ (qàngìmìz) *which* (one) *of us ?* قَنْغِیلَرِیكِزْ (qàngìlèrìnìz) *which* (ones) *of you ?* قَنْغِیلَرِی (qàngìlèrì) *which* (one, or, which ones) *of them ?*

نَه قَدْرْ or نَقَدَرْ (*vulg.* nìqàdàr) *how much ?*   نَه دُرْلُو (*vulg.* nè tùrlù) *what sort ?*   } are both substantives and adjectives.

SECTION VII. *The Relative Pronoun.*

THERE IS NO RELATIVE PRONOUN IN TURKISH, though attempts are made to use the Persian relative and conjunction, كِ (kì), as such, in literary composition. The Turkish *conjunction* كِ is a very different thing. Its use by Europeans

peans and others, as a relative pronoun, is greatly to be
avoided. This avoidance of all use of the relative pronoun
is the prime distinction of Turkish from all Aryan and Semitic
tongues. It is the perfection of language.

The numerous active and passive participles of the Turkish
verb obviate the necessity of a relative. The active participles take the place of our relative when it is nominative
to a verb; and the passive participles do so when our relative
is the accusative, or any indirect object of a verb. (See this
explained in the paragraphs on the Participles, in Section VIII.,
on the Verb.)

There is a peculiar Turkish relative, however, to which we
have no parallel in English,—the suffix ڴ (ki). It is attached
to nouns and pronouns substantive in two ways. If the substantive be in the genitive, the combination is a substantive,
and indicates *that which belongs to* (the substantive); thus,
بَابَا, بَابَانِك, بَابَانِڭكِى (bâbânìñkì) *the one which belongs to a* (or
the) father, بَابَامِڭكِى (bâbâmìñkì) *the one which belongs to my
father,* بَابَاسِنڭكِى (bâbâsìnìñkì) *the one belonging to his* (or *her*)
father, his father's one; &c. If the substantive be in the
locative case, the combination is sometimes a substantive,
sometimes an adjective. The substantive combination then
indicates *that which exists in* (the simple substantive); the
adjective combination expresses *the* (substantive) *which exists*

in (the first substantive). Thus, بَابَامْدَه‌كِى (bâbâmdèki) *the thing, the one that exists, that is in* (the possession or keeping of) *my father, which my father has* or *holds;* بَابَاسِنْدَه‌كِى عِلْم (bâbâsîndèki 'llfm) *the science possessed by his father, that is in his father.* The substantive combinations form the plural, and are declined ; the adjective combination is invariable.

With a noun of place or of time the same particle, كِى, forms a relative combination, substantive or adjective, having relation to the place or time named. In the case of the noun of place, the locative preposition may also be employed. Thus, أَشَاغِى *the foot,* or *lower part,* أَشَاغِيكِى and أَشَاغِيدَه‌كِى *that which is at the foot;* أَخْشَام *the evening,* أَخْشَامْ‌كِى *that which was* or *will be* (present) *in the evening.*

SECTION VIII.   *The Derivation of the Verb.*

As a general rule, each primary Turkish verb forms, itself included, a system of twelve *affirmative,* twelve *negative,* and twelve *impotential* verbs, by regular derivation ;—thirty-six in all ; one half being verbs *active,* the other half verbs *passive;* the active verbs being *transitive* or *intransitive;* the passives having for their nominative the direct or the indirect object of the transitive, the indirect object only of the intransitive primitive.

In another mode of subdivision, on the other hand, these

thirty-six verbs divide into two equal classes, in pairs, one of each pair being *simple*, and the other *causative* (which is also *permissive*, as the sense may show).

Each simple and causative pair of verbs is either *determinate*, *indeterminate*, or *reciprocal;* so that, by a special division of the same thirty-six, there are twelve determinate, twelve indeterminate, and twelve reciprocal verbs ; thus (giving the imperatives of each, for economy of space) :—

ACTIVE.

CLASSES.		TRANS. OR INTRANS. — Determinate.	TRANS. OR INTRANS. — Indeterminate.	INTRANSITIVE. — Reciprocal.
AFFIRMATIVE	Simple	نَپ (tèp) kick (him); kick.	تپن (tèpln) kick about, dance (in pain, with joy, &c.).	تپش (tèplsh) kick mutually one another.
	Causative (Permissive)	تپدر (tèpdlr) make or let (him) be kicked; ...kick.	تپندر (tèplndlr) make (him) kick about.	تپشدر (tèplshdlr) make (them) kick mutually one another.
NEGATIVE	Simple	تپمه (tèpmä) kick (him) not; kick not.	تپلمه (tèplnmä) kick not about.	تپشمه (tèplshmä) kick not mutually one another.
	Causative (Permissive)	تپدرمه (tèpdlrmä) make or let not (him) be kicked; ...kick.	تپندرمه (tèplndlrmä) make not (him) kick about.	تپشدرمه (tèplshdlrmä) make (them) not kick one another mutually.
IMPOTENTIAL	Simple	تپه مه (tèpèmä) be unable to kick (him); ... to kick.	تپنه مه (tèplnèmä) be unable to make (him) kick about.	تپشه مه (tèplshèmä) be unable to kick one onother mutually.
	Causative (Permissive)	تپدره مه (tèpdlrèmä) be unable to make (him) be kicked; ...kick.	تپندره مه (tèplndlrèmä) be unable to make (him) kick about.	تپشدره مه (tèplshdlrèmä) be unable to make (them) kick one another mutually.

PASSIVE.

INTRANSITIVE.

CLASSES.		Determinate.	Indeterminate.	Reciprocal.
AFFIRMATIVE	Simple	نُبَل (tĕpĭll) be kicked, be kicked in, &c.	نُبَل (tĕpĭnll) be kicked about in, &c.	نُبَل (tĕpĭshll) be mutually kicked in, &c.
	Causative (Permissive)	نُبِّرل (tĕpдĭrĭll) be made to be kicked.	نُبِّرل (tĕpĭndĭrĭll) be made to be kicked about in.	نُبِّرل (tĕpĭshdĭrĭll) be made to kick mutually one another.
NEGATIVE	Simple	نُبَلمَ (tĕpĭllmä) be not kicked.	نُبَلمَ (tĕpĭnllmä) be not kicked about in.	نُبَلمَ (tĕpĭshllmä) be not mutually kicked in.
	Causative (Permissive)	نُبِّرلمَ (tĕpдĭrĕlmä) be not made to be kicked.	نُبِّرلمَ (tĕpĭlodĭrĭlmä) be not made to be kicked about in.	نُبِّرلمَ (tĕpĭshdĭrĭlmä) be not made to mutually kick one another.
IMPOTENTIAL	Simple	نُبَلمَه (tĕpĭllĕmĕ) be unable to be kicked.	نُبَلمَه (tĕpĭnllĕmĕ) be unable to be kicked about in.	نُبَلمَه (tĕpĭshllĕmĕ) be unable to be mutually kicked in.
	Causative (Permissive)	نُبِّرلمَه (tĕpдĭrĭllĕmĕ) be unable to be made to be kicked.	نُبِّرلمَه (tĕpĭndĭlĭrĭllĕmĕ) be unable to be made to be kicked about in.	نُبِّرلمَه (tĕpĭshdĭrĭllĕmĕ) be unable to be made to mutually kick one another.

Remarks on the foregoing Table.

The imperative singular is the root, or simplest form in the conjugation, primitive or derivative, of the Turkish verb. This conjugation—unique for all the thirty-six forms, as will be seen further on—consists in adding certain vowels and consonants to the end of this conjugational root.

When the conjugational root of the simple affirmative form ends in ل, or in a vowel, it forms its passive by adding ن instead of ل. Thus : بُوْل (bûl) *find,* بُوْلُن (bûlûn, the ûtûrû dominating) *be found;* قَابْلَا (qâplâ) *cover,* قَابْلَان (qâplân) *be covered;* أُوقُو (ôqû) *read,* أُوقُون (ôqûn) *be read.* In the foregoing case of the vowel-ending, the passive sometimes takes both the ن and the ل, the ن always preceding; thus, قَابْلَانِل (qâplânîl, as قَابْلَان), *be covered,* أُوقُونُل (ôqûnûl, as أُوقُون) *be read.*

When the root of the simple affirmative has more than one syllable, and ends in ل, ر, or a vowel, its causative is formed by adding a letter ت in lieu of the syllable دِرْ. Thus, قِصَال (qîsâl) *become shorter,* قِصَالْت (qîsâlt) *make* or *let* (it) *become shorter; shorten* (it); أُوكْسُورْ (ûksûr) *cough,* أُوكْسُورْت (ûksûrt) *make* or *let* (him) *cough;* سُوَيْلَه (sûwéylé) *speak, say,* سُوَيْلَت (sûwéylât) *make* or *let* (him) *speak* or *say, make* or *let* (it) *be spoken* or *said* (by him); أُوقُو (ôqû) *read, recite,* أُوقُوت (ôqût) *make* or *let* (it) *be read* or *recited* (by him), *make* (him) *read.*

Many simple affirmative verbs ending in consonants also form their causatives in ر, preceded by a servile ésèrè, sometimes written یر, and even ور, with ûtûrû; not in در. No rule appears to exist on this subject, and the dictionary alone, or experience, can help the student in it. Thus, ايچ (îch) *drink* (it), اِچِیر (îchîr) or اِیچور (îchûr) *make* or *let* (it) *be drunk* (by him); بات (bât) *sink* (thou), باتِر (bâtîr) *make* or *let* (it) *sink, sink* (it); قاچ (qâch) *flee, escape,* قاچِر (qâchîr) *make* or *let* (him) *flee* or *escape.*

When the simple verb, affirmative, negative, or impotential, is transitive, its causative governs the same accusative ; and the nominative to the simple then becomes a dative to the causative. Thus, بَن اَنی یَازْدِم (bèn ânî yâzdîm) *I wrote it*, سَن اَنی بَكَ یَازْدِرْدِك (sâu ânî bâñâ yâzdîrdîñ) *thou madest it to be written by me* (thou causedst to me the writing it), *thou madest or lettest me write it.*

When the simple verb is neuter, its nominative becomes the accusative of its causative ; as, اُویُودُم (ûyûdûm) *I slept*, سَن بَنی اُویُوتْدُك (sân bènî ûyûtdûn) *thou madest or lettest me sleep.*

An indefinite series of causatives of every verb may be formed by repeating the causative suffixes, ت after در, and در after ت. They are sometimes useful, but are generally used in irony ; each augment adds an agent to the chain ; as, یَازْمَق,

H

يَازْدِرْدِرْمَقْ , يَازْدِرْتَدِرْمَقْ , يَازْدِرْمَقْ , &c.; this last means *to cause* (a thing) *to be caused* (by a second) *to be caused* (by a third) *to be written* (by a fourth agent).

The indeterminate is also called the *Reflexive* form. It has two uses. More generally it has the same intransitive signification with the simple form, as to the action, but betokens that this action is then performed without any determinate exterior object. Thus تِبِنْمَكْ is, *to kick one's feet or heels about as one lies or stands* (like a dancer, a man in a passion, a dying animal, &c.); بَاقِنْمَقْ (bàqlumàq) is, *to look about, here and there, in a perplexed or inquisitive manner;* &c. But, at other times, this form is transitive, and then indicates that the agent is either the direct or indirect object, also, of the action,—that the act is done to or for the agent's self. Thus, قِلِج قُوشَانْمَقْ (qïllj qùshànmàq) *to gird a sword on to one's self;* قَاشْنْمَقْ أَوْ اِیدِنْمَكْ (èv èdlumèk) *to acquire a house for one's self;* (qàshìnmàq) *to scratch one's self* (with one's nails); دِینْمَكْ (glylnmèk) *to put on one's clothes,* چِیزْمَه کِینْمَكْ (chìzmà glylnmèk) *to put on boots,* چِیزْمَلَرِیمِی کِینَیِم (chìzmàlèrìmi glylnèylm) *let me put on my boots;* &c.

Passive verbs of neuters are *defective;* they are conjugated in the third person singular only, and in inflexions over which person and number exercise no influence. They signify, *to be such that the neutral action takes place in, to, for, by, on account*

of, &c. (as expressed), something named, as the act of some or
any indeterminate agent. Thus, بویْـلَه تَپِنْلْمَز (bûylé tépinilmâz)
the act of kicking about is not thus performed, بورَادَه تَپِنْلْمَز (bûrâdâ
tépinilmâz) *the act of kicking about is not allowed here;* &c.
We have such passive verbs in English; as, *to be slept in, to
be fought for;* &c.

The Turkish passive verb always has, inherent in it, the
sense of *to be —able.* Thus, کَسِلُور (késilîr) *it is cut* (often),
it will be cut (then), *it is cuttable* (always); یَنْمَز (yénmâz) *it is
not eaten* (as a rule), *it will not be eaten* (then), *it is not eatable*
(either now, or by nature).

SECTION IX. *The Turkish Conjugation.*

All Turkish affirmative verbs, active or passive, transitive
or intransitive, are conjugated *in one and the same invariable
manner*, modified, as to their servile vowels and consonants,
by the laws of class and euphony alone. The negative and
impotential verbs differ from the affirmative, as to conjugation,
merely in the form of the aorist active participle, and of the
analogous aorist tense indicative. So that only one sole conjugation exists, in reality, in the Turkish language.

The conjugation consists of one simple and three complex
categories of moods, tenses, numbers, persons, participles,
verbal nouns, and gerunds; all four categories, simple and

complex, being fundamentally alike, but each modified in a certain special manner, to express a modified variation of the action.

Each category has six moods : the imperative, indicative, necessitative, optative (also subjunctive), conditional, and infinitive.

The imperative mood has one tense, the future.

The indicative has eight tenses, in four pairs ; the present and imperfect ; the aorist and past; the perfect and pluperfect; the future and past future.

The necessitative, optative, and conditional, have one pair each, the aorist and past. The infinitive has but one tense, the present.

Each category has five active participles; the present (which is the general active participle, applicable, in one sense, to any time, past, present, or future), the aorist, the past, the perfect, and the future. In Turkish, the present or active, the perfect or passive, are not confused together as in European languages ; each is distinct in form and in sense, and is different from the gerund in form, as it is, in grammar and in sense, different from the verbal noun.

The active participles of the passive verbs denote the direct recipients of the action of verbs transitive ; the passive participles of the same apply to the indirect objects thereof. The active participles of the passives of intransitives denote the indirect objects of the intransitive action; the passive participles of such passives are not in use.

Between the five active and two passive participles of each category, a Turkish conjugation thus furnishes twenty-eight participles for every verb, primitive or derivative. By the use of these numerous participles, it entirely avoids all necessity for a relative pronoun.

The present active participle adds an ûstûn and the letters اٰن, or only the letter ن, to the root that ends in a consonant; the aorist adds a vowel and the letters اٰر, or only the letter ر, with an ûstûn, رو with an ûtûrû, and ر only (or sometimes یر) with an êsêrê, for which no rule can be given; the past adds مِش (mish, mîsh) to all roots, whatever their ending; as the perfect adds دِك (dik) or دِق (dîq). The future adds an ûstûn and the letters ەجَك (êjêk) or ەجَق (âjâq) to consonantal roots, and یەجَك or یەجَق, with ûstûn, to vowel roots, including the negatives and impotentials. Thus, تَپَن (têpân), قِیرَان (qîrân) are present active participles; as, تَپِنَن (têpînân), تَپِشَن (têpî-shân), تَپِلَن (têpîlân), تَپِنِلَن (têpînilân), and تَپِشِلَن (têpishilân), are those of the simple affirmative derivatives. The causatives in دِر and in دِرل add the ûstûn and اٰن; while those in ت change it into د before the letters اٰن; thus, تَپْدِرَان (têpdirân), اۇتۇرْدَان (ótûrdân), تَپْدِرِلَن (têpdirilân), &c.; تَپْمِش (têpmish); تَپْدِك (têpdik); تَپَمَیەجَك (têpêjêk), تَپْمَیەجَك (têpmêyêjêk), تَپَمَیەجَك (têpdik);

(tèpèmèyèjèk), the final ı of the negative particle مه being elided as useless.

When the root ends with a vowel, as is the case with all the negatives and impotentials, the syllable يَانْ (yàn, yàn) is added in the present participle, the final ه or ى of the root being suppressed, and by some even the ا; but the و is kept intact. Thus, قَابْلَايَانْ or قَابِلَيَانْ (qàplàyàn), تَپْمَيَانْ (tèpmèyàn), تَبِنَهمِيَانْ (tèpìnèmèyàn), يُورُويَنْ (yùrùyàn), اُوقُويَانْ (òqùyàn).

The Turkish present active participle, in colloquial language, as a remanet from eastern Turkish, takes after it the preposition ده dè, dà, to form an adverb of past or future time; as, كِدَنْدَه (gìdàndè) when (I, thou, &c.) went, or shall go.

The aorist active participle, of the same form as the third person singular of the aorist tense of the indicative, always ends in a letter ر in affirmatives, and in the syllable مَزْ (màz) in negatives and impotentials. Thus, تَپَرْ (tèpèr), تَپْمَزْ (tèpmàz), تَپَمَزْ (tèpèmèz).

In the simple affirmative, the vowel added to the last consonant of the root, to which the final ر is then appended, cannot be defined by rule. Of course, it must be hard or soft according to the dominant in the root; but different verbs have ûstûn, others èsrè, others again ùtùrù, for their vowel; and with the ûstûn, all hard verbs add ا, as do some soft verbs; while other soft verbs dispense with this letter. Thus we have: قِرَار (qìrâr), كِيدَر (gldér), صَانُور (sânûr, *vulg.* sânìr),

كُور (gêlûr, *vulg.* gêlìr), صِيرِر (sìyìrìr).

The simple reflexive forms its aorist in ûtûrû and ور (gene-rally pronounced as êsérê and ـِر). The simple reciprocal does the same. We have, therefore, تِپِنُور (tèpìnûr, *vulg.* tèpìnìr), تِپِشُور (tèpìshûr, *vulg.* tèpìshìr). All the simple and causative passives follow this rule; thus, تِپِـلُور (tèpìlûr, tèpìlìr), تِپِنِلُور (tèpìnìlûr, tèpìnìlìr), تِپِشِلُور (tèpìshìlûr, tèpìshìlìr); تِپْدِرِلُور (tèp-dìrìlìr), تِپِنْدِرِلُور (tèpìndìrìlìr), تِپِشْدِرِلُور (tèpìshdìrìlìr). It will be observed that a vowel ی is intercalated before the ل in these words. This is a mechanical rule. The preceding ر is a letter that does not join on to its follower; this is the sole reason for the addition of that ی, when the following ل has a vowel. The same rule is applied by many to the ر of the causative ـِر, in like cases; that is, when it has its vowel, as it always has in the aorist. The words above given may therefore be written, تِپْدِرِیلُور ، تِپِنْدِرِیلُور ، تِپِشْدِرِیلُور; but this has no effect on the pronunciation.

The aorist passive participle has the same form as the active perfect, and the future passive is identical in form with the future active: تِپْدِك (tèpdìk); تِپَجَك (tèpéjèk).

There are three verbal nouns; the present or general, formed by adding مَه (mè, mâ) to the root, exactly like the negative imperative; the perfect, identical in form with the perfect active and aorist passive participles ; and the future, identical with the two future participles. Thus, تَپْمَه (tèpmè); تَپْدِكْ (tèpdìk) ; تَپَهجَكْ (tèpèjèk). The form تَپْمَه (tèpmè) of the present verbal noun is also that of a verbal adjective passive, signifying *done, made, effected as the result of* (the action of the verb); thus, تَپْمَه, as such adjective, means *caused by a kick or kicks.*

This derivative of the transitive verb active simple and causative can also take the passive sense ; thus, كَسْمَه (kèsmè), which naturally means *an act of cutting*, often means also *an act of being cut;* as, كَسْمَسِى قُولَاىْ (kèsmèsi qòlày) *it is easily cut.* It is also much used as a passive adjective when the verb is transitive ; as, اِينْجَه كَسْمَه تُوتُنْ (ìnjè kèsmè tùtùn) *finely cut tobacco;* and as an active adjective when the verb is intransitive ; as, بَابَادَنْ قَالْمَه مَالْ (bàbàdàn qàlmà màl) *property remaining from* (one's) *father.*

Leaving the gerunds for the present, we may now inquire into the mode of formation of the tenses of each mood. But before doing so, we must indicate the differences that serve clearly to distinguish the active participles, the passive participles, and the verbal nouns, of the two forms in دِكْ or دِقْ, and in دَجَكْ or دَجَقْ.

In the first place, the participles are adjectives, while the verbal nouns are substantives. Therefore, whenever a derivative in either of those forms qualifies a substantive, it must be a participle; it cannot be a verbal noun.

Secondly, the active participle qualifies the name of its actor only. It is therefore always a simple and invariable word, like the other active participles; as, أُورَايَه كِنْدِك آدَمْ وَارْمِى is there any man who has gone there? كِيدَهجَك سَنِّى سِين art thou he who is to go?

Thirdly, the passive participle always qualifies the name of the direct object, or of the indirect object, of the action, and is always accompanied by a possessive pronoun indicating the actor of that action. The first of these two facts distinguishes the passive participle from the verbal noun; the second distinguishes it from the active participle of the same form. Thus, أُوقُودُيغُمْ كِتَابْ (ôqûdûghûm kîtâb) *the book which I read* (now or formerly); أُوقُويَهجَغِمْ كِتَابْ (ôqûyâjâghîm kîtâb) *the book which I am going to read.* These are instances of the direct object qualified. So, أُوقُودُيـغُمْ زَمَان (ôqûdûghûm zêmān) *the time in which* (i. e. *when*) *I read;* and كِتَابِى أُوقُويَهجَغِمْ مَجْلِسْ (kîtâbî ôqûyâjâghîm mêjlîs) *the meeting in which I am going to read the book,* are instances of indirect objects; as is also أُويُويَهجَغِمْ أُوطَه (ûyûyâjâghîm ôdâ) *the room in which I am going to sleep.*

As instances of the substantival nature of the verbal nouns, let us take, يَازِى يَازْدِيغِمِى كُورْدِيكِزْمِى (yâzî yâzdîghîmî gyûrdûnûzmǔ) *have you seen my past action of writing writing ?* i. e., *have you ever seen me write ?* كَدَجَكِمِى كِـيمْ سُوَيْلَدِى (gálèjèyĭmĭ kĭm sǔwèylèdĭ) *who mentioned my future action of coming ?* i. e., *who told* (you, him, &c.) *that I was about to come ?*

Proceed we now to discuss the formation of the tenses.

The third person singular is the root of each tense, except in the imperative. Leaving the numbers and persons for future consideration, we may say, in the first place, that, as the second tense in each pair, of every mood (excluding the imperative and the infinitive), is formed from the first tense of the pair by the addition of the auxiliary اِيدِى (ĭdĭ) *was,* after it, we may leave these second tenses also for future con sideration.

By these means we arrive at the conclusion that there are four tenses in the indicative, and one each in the necessitative, optative, conditional, and infinitive, the forms of which have to be defined.

The four indicative tenses are—the present, the aorist (present habitual and future promissive), the perfect, and the future ; the single tense of the other three moods is their aorist (present or future); and that of the infinitive is its present.

The present indicative adds an èsèrè and the syllable يُورْ (yòr) to the consonantal root; thus, تَيُورْ (tèpĭyòr). It indicates a present action (actual or habitual); *he is kicking* (now); *he now habitually kicks.* Add the auxiliary ایدی to this, تپیورْ ایدی (tèpìyòr ìdì), and it forms the imperfect, *he was kicking* (then). A final ت more frequently changes to د; as, ایدیُورْ, اِیتْمَكْ (èdìyòr); کیدیُورْ, کِتْمَكْ (gìdìyòr); &c.

The aorist indicative varies in form of the servile syllable, but always ends in رْ in the affirmatives, and in مَزْ (mèz, màz) in the negatives and impotentials, being identical with the active aorist participle. It indicates a present *habit* (not a present *action*), or a future *assurance*, a future *promise*, as the context or circumstances may require. Thus, تپَرْ (tèpèr) *he kicks; he shall* or *will kick;* قیرَارْ (qìràr) *he breaks; he shall* or *will break;* یُورُورْ (yùrùr) *he walks; he will walk;* اُوقُورْ (òqùr) *he reads; he will read;* اِصِررْ (ìsìrìr) *he bites; he will bite;* تپْمَزْ (tèpmàz) *he does not kick; he will not kick;* تپَمَزْ (tèpèmèz) *he cannot kick.* The auxiliary ایدی, added to this, forms the past tense (showing a past *habit,* or an unfulfilled *condition*); تپَرْ ایدی (tèpèr ìdì) *he used to kick; he would kick* (if he could); *he would have kicked* (had he been able); in which two last senses, the expression is a virtual negative : *he kicks not,* because he is not able; *he did not kick,* because he was not able; تپْمَزْ ایدی (tèpmàz ìdì) *he used not to kick; he would not kick* (if he could); *he would not have kicked* (had he been able); تپَمَزْ ایدی (tèpèmèz ìdì) *he used not to be able to kick; he would*

not be able to kick (if so and so) ; *he would not have been able
to kick* (had not so and so); &c.

The perfect indicative is formed by adding the syllable دی
(dĭ, dĭ), in all cases, to the root. It is used in a determinate,
and also in an indeterminate past sense, referring the action to
a given past time, or to all past time. Thus, تَپْدِی (tĕpdĭ) *he
kicked* (then) ; *he has kicked* (without defining when). Add
the auxiliary ایدی, and the pluperfect results : تَپْدِی ایدی (tĕpdĭ
ĭdĭ), or تَپْدِیدِی (tĕpdĭdĭ), *he had kicked ;* تَپْمَدِی ایدی *he had not
kicked ;* تَپَمَدِی ایدی *he had not been able to kick.*

The future indicative is identical in form with the active
and passive future participles, and with the future verbal
noun. It indicates that the action expressed by the conjugational root is about to take place; thus, تَپَهجَك *he is about to
kick, he is going to kick ;* تَپْمَیَهجَك *he is not going to kick ;*
تَپَمَیَهجَك *he will not be able to kick.* Add the auxiliary ایدی,
and the past future results تَپَهجَك ایدی *he was going to kick,*
تَپْمَیَهجَك ایدی *he was not going to kick ;* تَپَمَیَهجَك ایدی *he was
unable to be about to kick.* Final ت in the root generally
changes to د , and a final vowel requires the addition of a consonant ی : یُورُویَهجَك , ایدَهجَك.

The aorist necessitative is formed by adding the syllables
مَلُو (mĕlĭ, mălĭ) to the root. It indicates a present duty to
perform a future act; and corresponds with our *must* or *ought.*

Thus, تَپْمَلُو *he must kick, he ought to kick;* تَپْمَمَلُو *he must not kick, he ought not to kick;* تَپَمَاملُو *he ought not to be able to kick.* With the auxiliary ايدى, we have the past necessitative, تَپْمَلُو ايدى *he ought to have kicked, he should have kicked;* تَپَمَامَلُو ايدى *he ought not to have kicked;* تَپَمَاملُو ايدى *he ought not to have been able to kick.*

The aorist optative is formed by adding an ûstûn and vowel ه to a consonantal root, or a syllable يَه (yė, yå) to a vowel root. Sometimes ١ is used in place of ه. The tense is a quasi-imperative, implying optation, or it is a subjunctive. Thus, تَپَه (tėpė) *let him kick, may he kick;* (that) *he may kick;* تَپْمَيَه (tėpmėyė, with suppression of the ه of the negation) *let him not kick, may he not kick;* (that) *he may not kick;* تَپَمَيَه (tėpėmėyė) *may he not be able to kick;* (that) *he may not be able to kick.* Add now the auxiliary ايدى, and we form the past tense, a virtual negative, expressive of regret; thus, تَپَه ايدى (tėpė ȋdȋ, more frequently written and pronounced تَپَيْدى tėpėydȋ) *had he kicked, if he had kicked; O that he had kicked;* تَپْمَيَيْدى (tėpmėyėydȋ) *had he not kicked, if he had not kicked; O that he had not kicked;* تَپَمَيَيْدى (tėpėmėyėydȋ) *had he not been able to kick, if he had not been able to kick; O that he had not been able to kick.*

The aorist conditional is formed by adding the syllable سَه (sė, så) to any root, consonantal or vowel. This performs the function of our conjunction *if*, in appearance; but, as أَكَرْ (èyèr), *if*, can be placed before it, it really is a subjunctive tense-ending. As a present, it admits the possibility of the action; as a future, it virtually denies the occurrence. Thus, تَپْسَهْ (tèpsè) *if he kick, if he were to kick;* تَپْمَسَهْ (tèpmèsè, the ۱ of negation elided) *if he kick not, were he not to kick;* تَپَمَسَهْ (tèpèmèsè) *should he not be able to kick.* Sometimes it is desiderative, *O that he kick!* &c. With ایدی added, we have the past conditional, which is always a virtual negative. Thus, تَپْسَیْدِی (tèpsèydì, for تَپْسَه‌ایدی) *had he kicked, if he had kicked;* تَپْمَسَیْدِی (tèpmèsèydì) *had he not kicked;* تَپَمَسَیْدِی (tèpèmèsèydì) *had he not been able to kick.*

The present of the infinitive is formed by adding مَكْ (mèk) or مَقْ (måq) to any root. Thus, تَپْمَكْ (tèpmèk) *to kick;* قَابْلَامَقْ (qåplåmåq) *to cover.* The negative and impotential are frequently written with ۱, and sometimes without a vowel-letter to end the root; as, تَپْمَامَكْ , تَپْمَمَكْ (tèpmèmèk), for تَپْمَهْ‌مَكْ ; تَپَمَامَكْ , تَپَمَمَكْ (tèpèmèmèk), for تَپَمَهْ‌مَكْ ; قَابْلَامَمَقْ (qåplåmå-måq), قَابْلَایَمَمَقْ (qåplåyåmåmåq). This tense is often rendered in English by the verbal noun in *-ing;* as, كِتْمَكْ قَالْمَقْدَنْ اوْلَی (gìtmèk qålmåqdån èvlå) *going is better than staying.* It also takes the suffix لِكْ , لِقْ after it to form an equivalent to our verbal noun in *-ing;* as, كِتْمَكْلِكْ *an act of going.*

There are seven *gerunds,* one *gerund-like verbal locution* of cause, one of verbal proportion, and six to indicate various times in relation with the action. All of these gerunds and gerund-like locutions presuppose the occurrence of two actions expressed in the sentence, one by the gerund, the other by a subsequent verb. The gerunds are a kind of verbal conjunctions, while the gerund-like locutions are verbal adverbs.

The first gerund, the most frequently used, ends in an ûtûrû, followed by ـُوب (ûb, ûb) after a consonant, or by يُوب (yûb, yûb) after a vowel. It indicates that two actions are being mentioned, of which the one implied by the gerund is prior as to time or natural sequence. We more usually, in English, express this relation of two actions by the conjunction *and*, though we occasionally use our gerund in *-ing*, as the Turkish does. Thus, تَپُوب قِرَار (tépûb qîrâr) *he kicks and breaks, will kick and break* (it) ; or, *kicking* (it), *he will break* (it). Conversationally, this gerund is pronounced with éséré in lieu of ûtûrû ; and with *p* in place of ـب ; as, tépîp, qîrîp, &c.

The second gerund is formed by adding ûstûn, and the letters ـه رَك (érék) or ـه رَق (ârâq), to a consonantal root, يَرَك (yérék) or يَرَق (yârâq) to a vowel-root. It is sometimes used in lieu of the first gerund, to obviate its too frequent recurrence ; but its distinctive use is to indicate that, of two contemporary sustained actions expressed, the one, subsidiary, accompanies the other. Thus, تَپَرَك كِتْدِى *kicking, he went off;* i. e., *he*

went off, kicking away (all the time) ; كُولَدِرَك گَلْدِى *he came,*
laughing (all the time).

The third gerund, in نجه (ĭnjė, ĭnjâ), after a consonant, or
يِنجَه (yĭnjė, yĭnjâ) after a vowel, and the fourth (used in writing
only, and much more rarely), in يِجَك (ijėk) or يِجَق (ĭjâq) after
a consonant, يِيجَك (yĭjėk) or يِيجَق (yĭjâq) after a vowel, has the
sense that its action is to be a kind of signal for the occurrence of the other expressed in the sentence ; it may, then, be
rendered by our *on* ... (with a gerund), also by our *as soon as*
... (with a verb). Thus, كُورنجَه تَپْدِى (gyŭrŭnjė tėpdĭ) *on seeing*
(him), *he kicked* (him) ; وَاصِلْ اُولِيِجَق مَعْلُومْ اُولَه (vāsĭl ŏlijâq, mâ‘-
lūm ŏlâ) *on reaching* (as soon as it reaches), *be* (it) *known*
(that......).

The fifth gerund is identical in form with the aorist optative, repeated. It expresses repetition of one act as a means
to the performance of a second. Thus, تَپَه تَپَه قِرْدِى (tėpė tėpė
qĭrdĭ), *kicking*, (and) *kicking* (it), *he broke* (it).

The sixth gerund is the infinitive with ėsėrė and يِن added ;
the Persian ک softened into Turkish ک (y value), and the ق
into غ. It expresses the verbal reason precedent for the
second action. Thus, أو تَپْمَكِين بَنْ قَاچْدِمْ *he kicking, I fled* ;
i. e., *because he kicked, I fled.*

The seventh gerund expresses the beginning of a time com-
mencing with the occurrence of an action and lasting until

now, during which another action has repeatedly or con-
tinuously occurred; it is equivalent to our *ever since* .....
In form it is the fifth gerund (not repeated) with the syllable
لُو (lú) or لِى (lï) added to it. Thus, تَپَلُو اَقْصَايُرْ (tèpèlú áqsáyòr)
ever since he kicked, he has limped.

The causal gerund-like locution is equivalent to the sixth
gerund in sense. It is the infinitive, with its final consonant
softened down, and with the preposition اِيلَه (ïlè, ïlä) added,
and shortened into لَ (lè, lä). Thus, تَپْمَكَّ (tèpmèylè) *by kicking.* No agent of the verb is then expressed in the verb,
though it be so exteriorly; as, بَنْ تَپْمَكَّ *by my kicking, I kicking.* There is another form into which this idea is cast, and
in which a perfect verbal noun, with a suffixed possessive pronoun indicative of the agent, and the ablative preposition دَنْ
(dän) are employed. Thus, تَپْدِيكِمْدَنْ (tèpdïyïmdän) *by my
(past) act of kicking.* This pronoun varies as is required:
تَپْدِيكِكْدَنْ (tèpdïyïñdän) *by thy act of kicking;* &c.

The gerund-like locution of verbal, i. e., of actional proportion is formed of the perfect active participle, with the
adverbial suffix of manner, جَه (jè, jä), added to it. It defines
a duration of time for two concurrent actions, the first circum-
scribing that duration for the continued or repeated occurrence
of the other; as, بَنْ تَپْدِكْجَه سَنْ طُوتْ (bèn tèpdïkjè, sän tút) *while
I kick, so long as I kick, do thou hold* (him). It sometimes

I

expresses the rate (proportion) of rapidity of the two actions;
as, وَقْت كَچِدِكْجَهِ اِيرِيلَشُورُ (wáqt gèchdìkjè, ìrìlèshìr) *as time goes by, it grows large* (larger).

The six verbal times indicated, in reference to an action, are the following: 1, the time before the action; 2, the time when the action is just about to occur; 3, the time while the action occurs; 4, the time when it occurred; 5, the time just when it has occurred; 6, the time after its occurrence. The first is the present verbal noun in the ablative; as, تَپْمَدَنْ (tèp-mèdèn), to which, for precision's sake, the adverb اَوَّلْ (ávvál) or مُقَدَّم (mùqáddàm), *anteriorly*, is subjoined. The expression تَپْمَدَنْ اَوَّلْ (or تَپْمَدَنْ اَوَّلْ), then, means *anteriorly to* (earlier than) *the action of kicking*; i. e., *before kicking*. Sometimes this is vulgarly expressed as تَپْمَزْدَنْ اَوَّلْ *before* (the agent) *kicks not*; i. e., *while* (as yet) *he has* (or *had*) *not kicked*.

The second gerund-like locution of time is the future active participle with the auxiliary gerund اِيكَنْ (ìkèn), *during*, added to it; thus, تَپَجَكْ اِيكَنْ *during* (the time of being) *about to kick*; i. e., *when just about to kick.*

The third is the aorist active participle with the same addition: تَپَرْ اِيكَنْ *during* (the time of being) *kicking*; i. e., *while kicking.*

The fourth is the perfect verbal noun or active participle, put in the locative (of time). It may be used impersonally,

with no addition in it ; and it may be used, for precision, with
the possessive pronoun of the agent between the verbal noun
and the preposition. In the former case, the verbal derivative
is possibly a participle ; in the latter, it is doubtlessly the
verbal noun. Thus, بَنْ تَپْدِكْدَه when *I* (became) *one who has
kicked* ; or بَنْ تَپْدِيكْمْدَه when *I* (performed) *my* (past) *act of
kicking* ; i. e., *when I kicked.*

The fifth is the past active participle with the auxiliary
اِيكَنْ ; as, تَپْمِشْ اِيكَنْ *during* (this time of the condition of)
having kicked ; i.e., *now that kicking has occurred, since* (*I*, &c.)
have kicked.

The sixth is the perfect verbal noun in the ablative (of
time), followed by the adverb صَكْرَه (sȯñrȧ, sȯrȧ), *after* ; thus,
تَپْدِكْدَنْ صَكْرَه (tėpdikdȧn sȯrȧ) *after the act of kicking.* The
possessive pronouns may be introduced into this locution before
the preposition ; as, تَپْدِيكْمْدَنْ صَكْرَه (tėpdiylmdȧn sȯrȧ) *after
my action of kicking.*

SECTION X. *The Numbers and Persons of the Verb.*

In all the tenses the first person singular is expressed by
the personal suffix م added to the verb, with ėsėrė given to the
tense-root, when this is a consonant ; and suppressing the final
ى of the tense-root where it occurs ; adding one where wanted.

It is wanting in the imperative. Thus : تَپِيُورِمْ (tèplyòrìm) *I am kicking* ; تَپِيُورْ اِيدِمْ (tèpyòr-ìdìm) *I was kicking* ; تَپَرِمْ (tèpè-rìm) *I kick; I shall or will kick* ; تَپَرْ اِيدِمْ (tèpèr-ìdìm) *I used to kick; I would kick; I would have kicked* ; تَپْدِمْ (tèpdìm) *I kicked; I did kick; I have kicked* ; تَپْدِيدِمْ (tèpdīdìm) *or* تَپْدِمْ اِيدِى (tèpdìm-ìdì) *I had kicked* ; تَپَجَكِمْ (tèpèjèyìm) *I am going to kick* ; تَپَجَكْدِمْ (tèpèjèkdìm) *I was going to kick* ; تَپْمَلُيِمْ (tèpmèllyìm) *I must kick* ; تَپْمَلُو اِيدِمْ (tèpmèll-ìdìm) *I should have kicked, ought to have kicked* ; تَپَمْ (tèpèm) *that I may kick* ; تَپَيْدِمْ (tèpèydìm) *that I had kicked* ; تَپْسَمْ (tèpsèm) *if I kick* ; تَپْسَيْدِمْ (tèpsèydìm) *if I had kicked.*

The second person singular, in all the tenses in دِى, is formed by changing the vowel ى into the nasal Turkish كْ ; as, تَپْدِكْ (tèpdìñ), تَپَرْ اِيدِكْ (tèpèr-ìdìñ), تَپِيُورْ اِيدِكْ (tèplyòr-ìdìñ), تَپَيْدِكْ (tèpèy-dìñ), تَپْمَلُو اِيدِكْ (tèpmèll-ìdìñ), تَپَجَكْ اِيدِكْ (tèpèjèk-ìdìñ), تَپْسَيْدِكْ (tèpsèydìñ). All the other tenses form it in سِنْ (sìñ), sometimes written and pronounced سِكْ (sìñ), excepting the present of the conditional, which forms it with سَكْ (sàñ, sàñ) ; sometimes written سَكْ, but pronounced like سَكْ. Thus, تَپِيُورْسِنْ (tèplyòrsìn), تَپَرْسِنْ (tèpèrsìn), تَپَجَكْسِنْ (tèpèjèksìn) ; تَپْمَلُوسِنْ (tèpmèllsìn), تَپَسِنْ (tèpèsìn).

The first person plural, likewise, in all the tenses in دِى, is

formed by changing the vowel ى into Arabic كْ (*k* value);
excepting that of the perfect, which, in hard words, always
forms this person in قْ instead of كْ. Thus, تَپْيُورْ اِيدِكْ (tèpiyŏr-
ĭdĭk), تَپَرْ اِيدِكْ (tèpèr-ĭdĭk), تَپْدِكْ (tèpdĭk), تَپْدِيدِكْ (tèpdīdĭk, or
تَپْدِكْ اِيدِى tèpdĭk-ĭdĭ), تَپَجَكْ اِيدِكْ (tèpèjèk-ĭdĭk, or تَپَجَكِيدِكْ
tèpèjèyĭdĭk, or تَپَجَكْدِكْ tèpèjèkdĭk), تَپْمَلُو اِيدِكْ (tèpmèlĭ-ĭdĭk),
تَپَيْدِكْ (tèpèydĭk), تَپْسَيْدِكْ (tèpsèydĭk). With a hard word like
بَاقْمَقْ (bāqmāq), the perfect forms بَاقْدِقْ (bāqdĭq). If this person in the past future indicative, in the past optative, and in
the past conditional, is used in the contracted form, these also,
with hard words, use قْ instead of كْ ; as, بَاقَه جَغْدِقْ (bāqàjàgh-
dĭq), بَاقَيْدِقْ (bāqàydĭq), بَاقْسَيْدِقْ (bāqsàydĭq). In the imperative
and present optative, it is formed by adding ûstûn and لِم to
the consonantal root, the syllable لِم having èsèrè for its vowel;
or, in vowel-roots, by adding the two syllables يَلِم (yèlĭm,
yàlĭm) ; thus, تَپَلِم (tèpèlĭm), بَاقَلِم (bāqàlĭm), سُوَيْلَيَهْ لِم (sûwèy-
lèyèlĭm), أُوقُويَهْ لِم (ŏqùyàlĭm, for لِم أُوقُويَهْ). In hard words, the
present of the conditional forms this person with قْ also; as,
بَاقْسَقْ (bāqsàq, sometimes written بَاقْسَقْ), أُوقُوسَقْ (ŏqùsàq,
أُوقُوسَقْ). The present, aorist, and future indicative, with the
present necessitative, form it in زْ or يِزْ, with èsèrè added to
the final consonant of the tense-root of the indicatives, and
with that vowel given to the ى of يِزْ in the necessitative;

thus, تِپِيُورِزْ (téplyórIz), تَپَرِزْ (tépérIz), تَپَجَكِزْ (tépéjéyIz, the
Arabic ك changed into Turkish ك, y value), تَپْمَلُوِيزْ (tépmé-
liylz). In hard words, the future indicative is in غ (softened
ق), with éséré before the final زْ ; as, بَاقَجَغِزْ (báqájághIz).

The second person plural, again, in all the tenses in دِى , is
formed in دِيكِزْ (dIñIz ; which is hard in the perfect of hard
words, dIñIz). Thus, تَپِيُورْدِيكِزْ (téplyórdIñIz), تَپَرْدِيكِزْ (tépér-
dIñIz), تَپْدِيكِزْ (tépdIñIz), بَاقْدِيكِزْ (báqdIñIz), تَپْدِيدِيكِزْ (tépdI-
dIñIz), تَپَجَكْدِيكِزْ (tépéjeydIñIz), تَپْمَلُو اِيدِيكِزْ (tépméll-IdIñIz),
تَپَيْدِيكِزْ (tépéydIñIz), تَپْسَيْدِيكِزْ (tépséydIñIz). The imperative
has two forms, in ك and ن كِزْ, both preceded by éséré, and a
consonant ى in vowel-roots ; as, تَپِكْ (téplñ), تَپِكِزْ (téplñIz,
written also تَپِيكِزْ) ; يَانِكْ (báqlñ), بَاقِكِزْ (báqlñIz);
قَاپْلَايِكْ (qápláyIñ), أُوقُويُنكُزْ (óqúyúñúz ; the útúrú dominating). All
the other tenses form it in سِيكِزْ (sIñIz, sIñIz), except the
present conditional, which has ústún for its first vowel, often
written سَكِزْ (sáñIz, sáñIz, to distinguish it better). Thus,
تَپَجَكْسِيكِزْ (tépéjék-sIñIz, تَپَرْسِكِزْ (tépérsIñIz), تَپِيُورْسِكِزْ (téplyórsIñIz),
sIñIz ; hard in hard words, بَاقَجَقْسِيكِزْ báqájáqsIñIz),
تَپْمَلُوسِنكِزْ (tépméllsIñIz), تَپَسِيكِزْ (tépéslñIz ; hard in hard words, بَاقَسِيكِزْ
báqásIñIz), تَپْسَكِزْ (tépséñIz; hard in hard words, بَاقْسَكِزْ báqsáñIz).
The third person plural is formed from the same person of

the singular, with the syllable لَر (lèr, lâr) added. Thus, تَپْسُوتْلَر
(tèpsinlèr); تَپِيُورْلَر (tèplyòrlâr), تَپَرْلَر (tèpèrlèr), تَپْدِيلَر (tèpdìlèr),
تَپَجَكْلَر (tèpèjèklèr), تَپْمَلِيلَر (tèpmèlìlèr), تَپَلَر (tèpèlèr), تَپْسَلَر
(tèpsèlèr). The tenses in اِيدِى may be formed in this way,
اِيدِى becoming اِيدِيلَر (ìdìlèr); or, the plural sign may be given
to the radical element, and اِيدِى be kept unchanged ; as,
تَپِيُورْ اِيدِيلَر or تَپِيُورْلَرِ اِيدِى ; and so throughout, except the past
optative, which prefers دِيلَر.

SECTION XI. *Of the Complex Categories.*

The Complex Categories of every Turkish verb, active or
passive, transitive or intransitive, affirmative, negative, or impotential, are formed, even as to their roots, with an auxiliary
verb, أُولْمَقْ (òlmâq) *to be or become;* itself conjugated, as a
simple verb, in conformity with what has already been laid
down, and joined to the aorist, past, and future active participles of the verb of which the complex category is to be
formed. The auxiliary follows the participle.

With the aorist participle, the auxiliary verb أُولْمَقْ forms
the First Complex Category; with the past participle, it forms
the Second Complex Category; and with the future participle,
it forms the Third Complex Category.

It would be possible to avoid using these terms, and to fuse

the whole into one vast conjugation, by following the method
used by European grammarians, each for the European language in which he treats of the subject. In some respects,
such an arrangement would possess an advantage. It would
bring together tenses of the one verb, which are but delicate
modifications of each other. The disadvantage would be, on
the whole, preponderant ; for the one vast conjugation of
simple and complex tenses formed with continually inter-
mingling, varying participles, would be very puzzling to the
novice, would choke out of view the principles of the subdivision, and prevent a lucid exposition thereof, besides
demanding the invention of a host of new names by which
to distinguish the numerous tenses so brought together ;
whereas, by keeping the same names for the same tenses of
the four categories, it would seem that a truer perception
of the shade of meaning which distinguishes each of the four
tenses of each name will be more easily attained and more
firmly grasped. Still, as a comparison with other systems
offers a certain amount of utility, we have given below the
three complex categories apart, to show their principles, and
have then arranged the whole four categories as a single conjugation.

Section XII. *The First Complex Category.*

This is formed with the aorist active participle, of every

class of verb, active or passive, transitive or intransitive, primary or derivative, affirmative or negative. In form, it is simply the conjugation of the auxiliary verb اُولْمَقْ (ólmáq) *to be,* the participle, as an adjective, remaining invariable throughout. We give one person only in each tense.

Infinitive.

تَپَرْ اُولْمَقْ (tèpèr ólmáq)   To be a willing, natural, deter-
mined, constant, or habitual
kicker; to be kicking; to
kick (habitually).

Imperative.

تَپَرْ اُولْ (tèpèr ól)   Be thou kicking; kick thou
(habitually).

Indicative.

Present.

تَپَرْ اُولِيُورِمْ (tèpèr ólíyórìm)   I am continually kicking.

Imperfect.

تَپَرْ اُولِيُورْ اِيدِمْ (tèpèr ólíyór ìdìm)   I was continually kicking.

Aorist.

تَپَرْ اُولُورِمْ (tèpèr ólùrùm)   I am continually kicking; I
shall be ever kicking.

Past.

تَپَرْ اُولُورْ اِيدِمْ (tèpèr ólùr ìdìm)   I used to be always kicking;
I would be, *or* would have
been, always kicking.

Perfect.

تَپَرْ اُولْدُمْ (tèpèr òldùm)   I became a constant kicker.

Pluperfect.

تَپَرْ اُولْدُمْ اِيدِی (tèpèr òldùm ìdì)   I had been or become a constant kicker.

Future.

تَپَرْ اُولَهجَغِمْ (tèpèr òlàjàghìm)   I am about to become a constant kicker.

Future Past.

تَپَرْ اُولَهجَغْدِمْ (tèpèr òlàjàghdìm)   I was about to become a constant kicker.

Necessitative.

Aorist.

تَپَرْ اُولْمَلُويِمْ (tèpèr òlmàlìyìm)   I must be, or become, a constant kicker.

Past.

تَپَرْ اُولْمَلُو اِيدِمْ (tèpèr òlmàlìyìdìm) I ought to have been a constant kicker.

Optative.

Aorist.

تَپَرْ اُولَيِمْ (tèpèr òlàyìm)   That I may be a constant
kicker.

Past.

تَپَرْ اُولَيْدِمْ (tèpèr òlàydìm)   That I had been a constant
kicker.

Conditional.

Aorist.

تَپَرْ أُولْسَمْ (tèpèr ólsåm) Were I, should I become, a constant kicker.

Past.

تَپَرْ أُولْسَيْدِمْ (tèpèr ólsåydìm) Had I been a constant kicker.

Active Participles.

Present.

تَپَرْ أُولَانْ (tèpèr ólån) Who *or* which is, was, will be, a constant kicker.

Aorist.

تَپَرْ أُولُرْ (tèpèr ólùr) (*perhaps unused, as a cacophony.*)

Past.

تَپَرْ أُولْمِشْ (tèpèr ólmùsh) Who has been a constant kicker.

Perfect.

تَپَرْ أُولْدُقْ (tèpèr óldùq) Who was a constant kicker.

Future.

تَپَرْ أُولَهجَقْ (tèpèr ólåjåq) Who is to be a constant kicker.

Passive Participles.

Aorist.

تَپَرْ أُولْدُقْ (tèpèr óldùq) Who *or* which (a kicker) has constantly kicked.

Future.

تَپَرْ اُولَجَقْ (tépér ólájáq)   Who, which (I, &c.) am about
                                   constantly to kick.

Verbal Nouns.

Present.

تَپَرْ اُولْمَه (tépér ólmá)   The act of being (at any time)
                                   a constant kicker.

Perfect.

تَپَرْ اُولْدُقْ (tépér óldúq)   The act of having been (then)
                                   a constant kicker.

Future.

تَپَرْ اُولَجَقْ (tépér ólájáq)   The act of being about (now)
                                   to become (hereafter) a con-
                                   stant kicker.

Gerunds.

1st. تَپَرْ اُولُوبْ (tépér ólúp)   Being a constant kicker
                                   (and ......).

2nd. تَپَرْ اُولَرَقْ (tépér óláráq) Continuing to be a con-
                                   stant kicker (*so and so
                                   also occurs*).

3rd. تَپَرْ اُولُنْجَه (tépér ólúnjá) ⎫ As soon as —— becomes
                                      ⎬ (became, will become) a
4th. تَپَرْ اُولِيجَقْ (tépér ólíjáq) ⎭ constant kicker, ...

5th. تَپَرْ أُولَه أُولَه (tèper ólå ólå) By continually being a constant kicker, ...

6th. تَپَرْ أُولْمَغِين (tèpèr ólmåghin) By reason of being a constant kicker, ...

7th. تَپَرْ أُولَلِى (tèpèr ólålî) Ever since —— became (has been) a constant kicker, ...

SECTION XIII. *The Second Complex Category.*

Infinitive.

Present.

تَپِمِشْ أُولْمَق (tèpmish ólmåq) To have kicked.

Imperative.

Future.

تَپِمِشْ أُولْ (tèpmish ól) Be thou one who has kicked; have kicked.

Indicative.

Present.

تَپِمِشْ أُولِيُورِمْ (tèpmish ólîyórîm) I am, *or* am becoming, one who has kicked; I have kicked.

Imperfect.

تَپِمِشْ أُولِيُورِدِمْ (tèpmish ólîyórdîm) I was, *or* was becoming, one who has kicked.

Aorist.

تَپِمِشْ أُولُورِمْ (tèpmish ólårùm) I shall have kicked.

Past.

تَپْمِشْ اُولُورْدُمْ (tèpmish òlùrdùm)   I should have kicked.

Perfect.

تَپْمِشْ اُولْدُمْ (tèpmish òldùm)   I became one who had kicked, I had kicked.

Pluperfect.

تَپْمِشْ اُولْدُمْ اِیدِی (tèpmish òldùm ìdì)   I had become one who has kicked.

Future.

تَپْمِشْ اُولَهجَغِمْ (tèpmish òlàjàghìm)   I am about becoming one who has kicked; I am going to have kicked.

Future Past.

تَپْمِشْ اُولَهجَقْ اِیدِمْ (tèpmish òlàjàq ìdìm)   I was about to have kicked.

Necessitative.

Aorist.

تَپْمِشْ اُولْمَلُویِمْ (tèpmish òlmàllìyìm)   I must (now) have kicked (then).

Past.

تَپْمِشْ اُولْمَلُویِ اِیدِمْ (tèpmish òlmàllìy ìdìm)   I must (then) have (already) kicked (before).

Optative.

Aorist.

تَپْمِشْ اُولَهیِمْ (tèpmish òlàyìm, اولهم òlàm)   That I may have kicked.

Past.

تَپْمِشْ اُولَيْدِمْ (tĕpmĭsh ŏlȧydĭm)   That I had kicked.

Conditional.
Aorist.

تَپْمِشْ اُولْسَمْ (tĕpmĭsh ŏlsȧm, اولسم)   Had I kicked (then).

Past.

تَپْمِشْ اُولْسَيْدِمْ (tĕpmĭsh ŏlsȧydĭm)·   Had I (already) kicked
                                                (before then).

Active Participles.
Present.

تَپْمِشْ اُولَانْ (tĕpmĭsh ŏlȧn)   Who has (already) kicked.

Aorist.

تَپْمِشْ اُولُورْ (tĕpmĭsh ŏlȗr)   Who will have (already)
                                        kicked.

Past *and* Perfect, *perhaps not used.*

Future.

تَپْمِشْ اُولَجَقْ (tĕpmĭsh ŏlȧjȧq)   Who will become one who
                                          has kicked.

Passive Participles.
Aorist.

تَپْمِشْ اُولْدُقْ (tĕpmĭsh ŏldȗq)   Which (a kicker) had
                                          (already) kicked.

Future.

تَپمِش أُولَهجَّق (tèpmish ölåjåq)   Which (a kicker) will have kicked.

Verbal Nouns.

Present.

تَپمِش أُولْمَه (tèpmish ölmå)   The (present state of) having (already) kicked.

Perfect.

تَپمِش أُولْدُّق (tèpmish öldůq)   The (past state of) having (previously) kicked.

Future.

تَپمِش أُولَهجَّق (tèpmish ölåjåq)   The (future state of) having (previously) kicked.

Gerunds.

1st.   تَپمِش أُولُوب (tèpmish ölůp)   Having kicked (and....).

2nd.   أُولَهرَق   ... (...   ölåråq)   Having the continued quality of having kicked (and ...).

3rd.   أُولُنجَه   ... (...   ölůnjå)   As soon as (— is, was, will be) one who *or* which had kicked, ...

4th.   أُولِيجَق   ... (...   ölijåq)   The instant (—) had kicked, ...

5th. تَپْمِش أُولَه أُولَه (tĕpmĭsh ŏlắ ŏlắ)   By continuing to have kicked, ...

6th. أُولْمَغِين   ...   (...   ŏlmắghĭn) By reason of having kicked, ...

7th. أُولَدَلِى   ...   (...   ŏlắlĭ) Since — became one who had kicked, ...

Section XIV. *The Third Complex Category.*

Infinitive.
Present.

تَپَجَك أُولْمَق (tĕpĕjĕk ŏlmắq)   To be about to kick (ready to kick).

Imperative.
Future.

تَپَجَك أُولْ (tĕpĕjĕk ŏl)   Be thou about to kick.

Indicative.
Present.

تَپَجَك أُولِيُورِم (tĕpĕjĕk ŏlĭyŏrĭm)   I am (often) on the point of kicking; I become on the point ....

Imperfect.

تَپَجَك أُولِيُور اِيدِم (tĕpĕjĕk ŏlĭyŏr ĭdĭm)   I was (often) on the point ....

Aorist.

تَپَجَك أُولُورِم (tĕpĕjĕk ŏlúrúm)   I am (habitually), I shall be (then) on the point ...

K

Past.

تَپَهجَكْ اُولُورْدُمْ (tèpèjèk ólùrdùm)   I used (habitually); I should be (then) on the point ....

Perfect.

تَپَهجَكْ اُولْدُمْ (tèpèjèk óldùm)   I was (then) on the point ....

Pluperfect.

تَپَهجَكْ اُولْدُمْ اِيدِى (tèpèjèk óldùm ìdì)   I had been (before then) on the point ....

Future *and* Future Past.

تَپَهجَكْ اُولَهجَغِمْ (tèpèjèk óláj́ághìm)   ⎫
تَپَهجَكْ اُولَهجَغْدِمْ (tèpèjèk óláj́ághdìm)   ⎬ *Not used, as being caco-phonies.*
                                                ⎭

Necessitative.

Aorist.

تَپَهجَكْ اُولْمَلِيِمْ (tèpèjèk ólmàlìyìm)   I must be on the point ....

Past.

تَپَهجَكْ اُولْمَلِيِدِمْ (tèpèjèk ólmàlìyìdìm)   I ought to have been on the point ....

Optative.

Aorist.

تَپَهجَكْ اُولَمْ (tèpèjèk ólám)   That I may be on the point ....

Past.

تَپَجَك أُولَيْدِم (tèpèjèk òláydìm)   That I had been on the point ....

Conditional.

Aorist.

تَپَجَك أُولَسَم (tèpèjèk òlsàm)   Were I to be *or* become on the point ....

Past.

تَپَجَك أُولَسَيْدِم (tèpèjèk òlsàydìm)   Had I been on the point ....

Active Participles.

Present.

تَپَجَك أُولَان (tèpèjèk òlàn)   Who *or* which is *or* becomes on the point ....

Aorist.

تَپَجَك أُولُور (tèpèjèk òlùr)   Who *or* which is (naturally) *or* will be (some time) on the point ....

Past *and* Perfect.

تَپَجَك أُولْمُش (tèpèjèk òlmùsh) ⎫
تَپَجَك أُولْدُق (tèpèjèk òldùq) ⎬   Who *or* which has been *or* was (then) on the point....

Future.

تَپَجَك أُولَجَق (tèpèjèk òlàjàq)   *Not used, as being cacophonous.*

Passive Participles.

Aorist.

تَپَهجَك اُولَدُق (tèpèjèk òldùq)   Which (a kicker) was on the
point ....

Future.

Cacophonous ; not used.

Verbal Nouns.

Present.

تَپَهجَك اُولْمَه (tèpèjèk òlmà)   The act of being *or* becoming
(at any time) on the point....

Perfect.

تَپَهجَك اُولَدُق (tèpèjèk òldùq)   The past act *or* state of being
(then) on the point ....

Future.

Cacophonous ; not used.

Gerunds.

1st. تَپَهجَك اُولُوب (tèpèjèk òlùp)   Being about to kick
(and ....)

2nd. اُولَهرَق ... (... òlàràq)   Continuing to be about
to kick (and ....)

3rd. اُولُنْجَه ... (... òlùnjà)   As soon as (— is, was,
will be) about to kick,
......

4th. اُولِيجَن ... *Cacophonous.*

5th. اولَه اولَه تَپَجَك (tèpéjèk ólå ólå) By continuing to be about to kick, ...

6th. اولْمَغِين ... (... ólmåghìn) By reason of being about ....

7th. اولَـدلِى ... (... ólålí) Ever since — became on the point ....

Section XV. *The Combined (true Turkish) Conjugation.*

Infinitive.

Present.	تَپْمَك	تَپَرْ اولْمَق	تَپْمِش اولْمَق	تَپَجَك اولْمَق

Imperative.

Future.	تَپْ	تَپَرْاولْ	تَپْمِش اولْ	تَپَجَك اولْ

Indicative.

Present.	تَپْيُورْ	تَپَرْ اولِيُورْ	تَپْمِش اولِيُورْ	تَپَجَك اولِيُورْ
Imperf.	تَپْيُورْدِى	اولِيُورْدِى ...	اولِيُورْدِى ...	اولِيُورْدِى ...
Aorist.	تَپَرْ	اولُورْ ...	اولُورْ ...	اولُورْ ...
Past.	تَپَرْدِى	اولُورْدُى ...	اولُورْدُى ...	اولُورْدُى ...
Perfect.	تَپْدِى	اولْدُى ...	اولْدُى ...	اولْدُى ...
Pluperf.	تَپْدِيدِى	اولْدُيدُى ...	اولْدُيدُى ...	اولْدُيدُى ...
Future.	تَپَجَك	اولَه جَق ...	اولَه جَق ...	(*not used*)
Fut.Past.	تَپَجَكْدِى	اولَه جَقْدِى	اولَه جَقْدِى ...	(*not used*)

Necessitative.

Aorist.	تپهجك اُولَمَلِو	تپمِش اُولمَلِو	تپَر اُولَمَلِو	تپمَلِو
Past.	... اُولمَلِو ایدِی	... اُولْمَلِو ایدِی	...	تپمَلِو ایدی

Optative.

Aorist.	تپهجك اُولَه	تپمِش اُولَه	تپَر اُولَه	تپَه
Past.	... اُولَیدِی	... اُولَیدِی	... اُولَیدِی	تپَیدِی

Conditional.

Aorist.	تپهجك اُولسَه	تپمِش اُولسَه	تپَر اُولسَه	تپسَه
Past.	... اُولسَیدِی	... اُولسَیدِی	... اُولسَیدِی	تپسَیدِی

Active Participles.

Present.	تپهجك اُولان	تپمِش اُولان	تپَر اُولان	تپن (تپان)
Aorist.	... اُولُور	... اُولُور	... اُولُور	تپَر
Past.	... اُولمُش	(not used)	... اُولمُش	تپمِش
Perfect.	... اُولدُق	... اُولدُق	... اُولدُق	تپدك
Future.	(not used)	... اُولَه جَق	... اُولَه جَق	تپهجك

Passive Participles.

Aorist.	تپهجك اُولدُق	تپمِش اُولدُق	تپَر اُولدُق	تپدك
Future.	(not used)	... اُولَه جَق	... اُولَه جَق	تپهجك

Verbal Nouns.

Present.	تَپْمَه	تَپْرَاوُلْمَه	تَپْمِش اُولْمَه	تَپَهجَكْ اُولْمَه
Perfect.	تَپْدِكْ	... اُولْدُقْ	... اُولْدُقْ	... اُولْدُقْ
Future.	تَپَهجَكْ	... اُولَهجَقْ	... اُولَهجَقْ	(not used.)

... ...Gerunds.

1st.	تَپُوب	تَپْرَاوُلُوب	تَپْمِش اُولُوب	تَپَهجَكْ اُولُوب
2nd.	تَپَرَكْ	... اُولَهرَقْ	... اُولَهرَقْ	... اُولَهرَقْ
3rd.	تَپْنِجَه	... اُولُنْجَه	... اُولُنْجَه	... اُولُنْجَه
4th.	تَپْيِجَكْ	... اُولِيجَقْ	... اُولِيجَقْ	... اُولِيجَقْ
5th.	تَپَه تَپَه	... اُولَه اُولَه	... اُولَه اُولَه	... اُولَه اُولَه
6th.	تَپْمَكِين	... اُولْمَغِين	اُولْمَغِين	اُولْمَغِين
7th.	تَپَهلُو ...	... اُولَهلُو	... اُولَهلُو	... اُولَهلُو

SECTION XVI. *The Negative and Impotential Conjugations.*

The Negative and Impotential Conjugations, twenty-four in
number to each simple verb, as a general rule, are formed precisely on the lines of the simple affirmative conjugation in its
four categories, as above given, with the exception of the
aorist of the indicative, as to its root-word of the third person

singular, and the corresponding aorist active participle, which
end in مَز (máz), instead of the final ر of the affirmative.

Infinitive.
Present.

تَپَمَمَكْ	تَپْمَزْ اُولْمَقْ	تَپْمامِشْ اُولْمَقْ	تَپْمَيَجَكْ اُولْمَقْ
تَپَمامَكْ	تَپَمَزْ ...	تَپَمامِشْ ...	تَپَمَيَجَكْ ...

Imperative.
Future.

تَپْمَه	تَپْمَزْ اُولْ	تَپْمامِشْ اُولْ	تَپْمَيَجَكْ اُولْ
تَپَمَه	تَپَمَزْ...	تَپَمامِشْ...	تَپَمَيَجَكْ...

Indicative.
Present.

تَپْميُورْ	تَپْمَزْ اُوليُورْ	تَپْمامِشْ اُوليُورْ	تَپْمَيَجَكْ اُوليُورْ
تَپَميُورْ	تَپَمَزْ...	تَپَمامِشْ ...	تَپَمَيَجَكْ ...

Imperfect.

تَپْميُوردِى	تَپْمَزْ اُوليُوردِى	تَپْمامِشْ اُوليُوردِى	تَپْمَيَجَكْ اُوليُوردِى
تَپَميُوردِى	تَپَمَزْ ...	تَپَمامِشْ ...	تَپَمَيَجَكْ ...

Aorist.

تَپْمَزْ	تَپْمَزْ اُولُورْ	تَپْمامِشْ اُولُورْ	تَپْمَيَجَكْ اُولُورْ
تَپَمَزْ	تَپَمَزْ ...	تَپَمامِشْ ...	تَپَمَيَجَكْ ...

Past.

تَمِزْدِى	تَمِزْ اُولُورْدِى	تَمَامِشْ اُولُورْدِى	تَمِيَه جَكْ اُولُورْدِى
تَپَه مَزْدِى	تَپَه مَزْ ...	تَپَه مَامِشْ ...	تَپَه مِيَه جَكْ ...

Perfect.

تَمْدِى	تَمِزْ اُولْدِى	تَمَامِشْ اُولْدِى	تَمِيَه جَكْ اُولْدِى
تَپَه مَدِى	تَپَه مَزْ ...	تَپَه مَامِشْ ...	تَپَه مِيَه جَكْ ...

Pluperfect.

تَمْدِيدِى	تَمِزْ اُولْدِيدِى	تَمَامِشْ اُولْدِيدِى	تَمِيَه جَكْ اُولْدِيدِى
تَپَه مَدِيدِى	تَپَه مَزْ ...	تَپَه مَامِشْ ..	تَپَه مِيَه جَكْ ...

Future.

تَمِيَه جَكْ	تَمِزْ اُولَه جَقْ	تَمَامِشْ اُولَه جَقْ	(not used)
تَپَه مِيَه جَكْ	تَپَه مَزْ ...	تَپَه مَامِشْ ...	(not used)

Future Past.

تَمِيَه جَكْدِى	تَمِزْ اُولَه جَقْدِى	تَمَامِشْ اُولَه جَقْدِى	(not used)
تَپَه مِيَه جَكْدِى	تَپَه مَزْ ...	تَپَه مَامِشْ ...	(not used)

Necessitative.

Aorist.

تَمَامْلِو	تَمِزْ اُولْمَلِو	تَمَامِشْ اُولْمَلِو	تَمِيَه جَكْ اُولْمَلِو
تَپَه نَامْلِو	تَپَه مَزْ...	تَپَه مَامِشْ ...	تَپَه مِيَه جَكْ ...

Past.

تَمْیَەجَك اُولْمَلو ایدِی   تَمْامِش اُولْمَلو ایدِی   تَمِز اُولْمَلو ایدِی   تَمَاملو ایدِی

تَپَەمَیَەجَك ...   تَپَەمَامِش ...   تَپَەمَز ...   تَپَەمَاملو ایدِی

Optative.
Aorist.

تَمْیَەجَك اُولَه   تَمْامِش اُولَه   تَمِز اُولَه   تَمْیَە

تَپَەمَیَەجَك ...   تَپَەمَامِش ...   تَپَەمَز ...   تَپَەمَیَە

Past.

تَمْیَەجَك اُولَیْدِی   تَمْامِش اُولَیْدِی   تَمِز اُولَیْدِی   تَمْیِیْدِی

تَپَەمَیَەجَك ...   تَپَەمَامِش ...   تَپَەمَز ...   تَپَەمَییْدِی

Conditional.
Aorist.

تَمْیَەجَك اُولْسَه   تَمْامِش اُولْسَه   تَمِز اُولْسَه   تَمْسَه

تَپَەمَیَەجَك ...   تَپَەمَامِش ...   تَپَەمَز ...   تَپَەمَسَه

Active Participles.
Present.

تَمْیَەجَك اُولَان   تَمْامِش اُولَان   تَمِز اُولَان   تَمْیَان

تَپَەمَیَەجَك ...   تَپَەمَامِش ...   تَپَەمَز ...   تَپَەمَیَان

Aorist.

تَپْمَز	تَپْمَزْ اُولُوُرْ	تَپْمامِشْ اُولُوُرْ	تَپْمِيَەجَكْ اُولُوُرْ
تَپَەمَزْ	تَپَەمَزْ...	تَپَەمامِشْ ...	تَپَەمَيَەجَكْ ...

Past.

تَپْمامِشْ	تَـپْمَزْ اُولْمِشْ	(not used)	تَپْمِيَەجَكْ اُولْمِشْ
تَپَەمامِشْ	تَپَەمَزْ ...	(not used)	تَپَەمَيَەجَكْ ...

Perfect.

تَپْمَدِكْ	تَپْمَزْ اُولْدُقْ	تَپْمامِشْ اُولْدُقْ	تَپْمِيَەجَكْ اُولْدُقْ
تَپَەمَدِكْ	تَپَەمَزْ...	تَپَەمامِشْ ...	تَپَەمَيَەجَكْ ...

Future.

تَـپْمِيَەجَكْ	تَـپْمَزْ اُولَەجَقْ	تَپْمامِشْ اُولَەجَقْ	(not used)
تَپَەمَيَەجَكْ	تَپَەمَزْ ...	تَپَەمامِشْ ...	(not used)

Passive Participles.

Aorist.

تَپْمَدِكْ	تَـپْمَزْ اُولْدُقْ	تَـپْمامِشْ اُولْدُقْ	تَپْمِيَەجَكْ اُولْدُقْ
تَپَەمَدِكْ	تَپَەمَزْ ...	تَپَەمامِشْ ...	تَپَەمَيَەجَكْ ...

Future.

تَـپْمِيَەجَكْ	تَـپْمَزْ اُولَەجَقْ	تَپْمامِشْ اُولَەجَقْ	(not used)
تَپَەمَيَەجَكْ	تَپَەمَزْ ...	تَپَەمامِشْ ...	(not used)

Verbal Nouns.

Present.

تَـمَامَه	تَـمْز اُولْمَه	تَمَامِش اُولْمَه	تَـمْيَه جَك اُولْمَه
تَپَمَامَه	تَپَمَزْ...	تَپَمَامِش...	تَپَمَيَه جَك ...

Perfect.

تَمْدِك	تَمْز اُولْدُق	تَمَامِش اُولْدُق	تَمْيَه جَك اُولْدُق
تَپَمَدِك	تَپَمَزْ ...	تَپَمَامِش ...	تَپَمَيَه جَك ...

Future.

تَمْيَه جَك	تَمْز اُولَه جَق	تَمَامِش اُولَه جَق	(*not used*)
تَپَمَيَه جَك	تَپَمَزْ ...	تَپَمَامِش ...	(*not used*)

Gerunds.

1st.	تَمَيُوبْ / تَپَمَيُوبْ	تَـمْز اُولُوبْ / تَپَمَزْ ...	تَمَامِش اُولُوبْ / تَپَمَامِش ...	تَمْيَه جَك اُولُوبْ / تَپَمَيَه جَك ...
2nd.	تَمَيَرَك / تَپَمَيَرَك	تَمْز اُولَه رَق / تَپَمَزْ ...	تَمَامِش اُولَه رَق / تَپَمَامِش ...	تَمْيَه جَك اُولَه رَق / تَپَمَيَه جَك ...
3rd.	تَمَيِنْجَه / تَپَمَيِنْجَه	تَمْز اُولَنْجَه / تَپَمَزْ ...	تَمَامِش اُولَنْجَه / تَپَمَامِش ...	تَمْيَه جَك اُولَنْجَه / تَپَمَيَه جَك ...
4th.	تَمْيِيجَك / تَپَمَيِيجَك	تَمْز اُولِيجَق / تَپَمَزْ ...	تَمَامِش اُولِيجَق / تَپَمَامِش ...	تَمْيَه جَك اُولِيجَق / تَپَمَيَه جَك ...

5th.	تَبْمِيَه تَبْمِيَه	تَـبْمَرْ أُولَه أُولَه	تَبْمَامِشْ أُولَه أُولَه	تَبْمِيَهجَكْ أُولَه أُولَه
	تَبَمِيَه تَبَمِيَه	تَبَمَزْ ...	تَبَمَامِشْ ...	تَبَمِيَهجَكْ ...
6th.	تَبْمَامَكِينْ	تَـبْمَرْ أُولْمَغِينْ	تَبْمَامِشْ أُولْمَغِينْ	تَبْمِيَهجَكْ أُولْمَغِينْ
	تَبَمَامَكِينْ	تَبَمَزْ ...	تَبَمَامِشْ ...	تَبَمِيَهجَكْ ...
7th.	تَـبْمِيَهلُو	تَـبْمَرْ أُولَهلُو	تَبْمَامِشْ أُولَهلُو	تَـبْمِيَهجَكْ أُولَهلُو
	تَبَمِيَهلُو	تَبَمَزْ ...	تَبَمَامِشْ ...	تَبَمَامِشْ ...

SECTION XVII.

The Dubitative, Potential and Facile Verbs, &c.

The Dubitative Verb is formed by adding the syllable مِشْ (mǐsh, mísh), or the word اِيمِشْ (ímǐsh), to any personal verb, indicative or necessitative, active or passive, affirmative, negative, or impotential; but, in the perfect indicative, it displaces the syllable دِى (dǐ) of the root. It casts a doubt on what is said; and is often added, in conversation, by another speaker, to express that he considers what has been affirmed by the former speaker to be questionable, or hearsay, or mere assumption. When the first speaker uses it himself, he does so to express that what he relates is either doubtful, hearsay, or erroneous assumption, from some other person. It is a gross vulgarism, to which Armenians and European novices are addicted, to use this dubitative syllable, in conversation, where the دی of the perfect indicative, or of any compound tense, is required. In writing, there is no denying that this form is systematically used, by the best authorities, in place of the tense they would employ in speaking. The form has a more musical sound; and it is, in my opinion, a fruit of imitating Persian verb-forms in Turkish; initiated, probably, by the Persian scribes of the early reigns.

In dubitative conjugation, this syllable مِش follows the simple tense-root and its plural, preceding the compound and personal terminations, singular or plural; unless it be spoken by another person. In this last case, it naturally comes alone, after all other words. Thus : تَپِیُورْمِشِم (tèplyórmishìm) *it is said, supposed, pretended, suggested, &c., that I am kicking;* تَپِیُورْمِش اِیدِك (tèplyórmish ìdiñ) *it is said, &c., that thou wast kicking;* تَپَرَایِمِش (tèpèr ìmish) *it is said, &c., that he kicks;* تَپَرْمِش اِیدِك (tèpèrmish ìdik) *it is said, &c., that we used to kick;* تَپْمِش سِكِز (tèpmish sìñìz) *it is said, &c., that you kicked or have kicked;* تَپَجَكْرَایِمِش (tèpèjèklèr ìmish) *it is said, &c., that they are going to kick.* (This word or syllable, مِش, اِیمِش, is really the past active participle of the obsolete verb اِیمَك.)

The Potential Verb is formed of the fifth gerund (not repeated) followed by the verb بِلْمَك (bìlmèk) in its entire conjugation, the gerund remaining unchanged throughout. This auxiliary verb then means *to be able,* and answers to our

English *can.* Ex.: تَپَه بِلْمَك (tèpè bìlmèk) *to be able to kick ;*
تَپَه بِلِيُورِمْ (tèpè bìlìyòrìm) *I am able to kick, I can kick ;* &c.

The Facile Verb is formed by the root of a verb, to which an èsèrè is added, followed by a vowel ى and the auxiliary verb وِيَرْمَك (vìrmèk, *vulg.* vèrmèk). With a vowel verb other than one in ى, a consonantal ى, with èsèrè, is added between the root-vowel and the servile ى vowel; and with a verb in vowel ى, this is made into a consonant with èsèrè, and the servile vowel ى is then added; as, تَپِيوِيَرْمَك (tèpì-vìrmèk), قَاپْلَايِيوِيَرْمَك (qàplàyì-vìrmèk), أُوقُويُيوِيَرْمَك (òqùyù-vìrmèk), قَازِيِيوِيَرْمَك (qàzìyì-vìrmèk). The sense of these verbs is that of great ease, readiness, off-handedness in the action, which we express in English by saying *just to kick, just to give a kick; just to cover over; just to read* or *recite; just to scratch out;* &c.

· There are several other Turkish verbs in use as special auxiliaries after the gerund of the original verb; as, كَلْمَك (gàlmèk), دُورْمَق (dùrmàq), قَالْمَق (qàlmàq), يَاتْمَق (yàtmàq), and يَازْمَق (yàzmàq). The first expresses a frequent or natural happening; the next three signify persistency; and the last the idea of having almost happened, of being within an ace of happening. Thus, أُولَه كَلْمَك (òlà gàlmèk) *to happen frequently, of course, as is well known; to be a common occurrence;* بَاقَه قَالْمَق (bàqà dùrmàq) *to stand looking;* بَاقُوبْ دُورْمَق (bàqà qâlmâq) *to stand* (remain) *staring in surprise and amazement;*

دوشنوب ياتمق (dûshûnûp yâtmâq) *to remain* (lie) *pondering, in a brown study;* بايله يازمق (bâyîlâ yâzmâq) *to give one's self up* (write) *as about to faint;* &c., &c., &c.

Section XVIII. *The Verb Substantive.*

In Turkish there is no *extant* verb substantive, answering in all its moods and tenses to our verb *to be.* In one sense, the Turkish اولمق performs the office, as an auxiliary and as an independent verb; but as such, it is a verb adjective, and continually lapses into the parallel idea of *to become.*

The Turkish originally had a true verb substantive, ايمك (îmêk) *to be.* This exists fragmentarily in Ottoman Turkish; perhaps in certain persons of the present, certainly in the perfect of the indicative, in the aorist conditional, in the past active participle, in the perfect verbal noun, and in the gerund, apparently modified from the present active participle (which in eastern and old Turkish was and is formed in كان or غان, even قان, traces of which are numerous in Ottoman, as adjectives). Thus:

Indicative.

Present. ايم (îm, im), يم (yîm, yim) *I am;* سين (sîn, sin) *thou art;* ايز (îz, iz), يز (yîz, yiz) *we are;* سكز (sîñîz, sîñîz) *you are.*

Perfect. اِيدِم (ĭdĭm) *I was*, اِيدِك (ĭdĭñ) *thou wast*, اِيدِى (ĭdĭ)
he was; اِيدِك (ĭdĭk) *we were*; اِيدِيكِز (ĭdĭñĭz) *you were*;
اِيدِيلَـر (ĭdĭlér) *they were*.

Conditional Aorist.

اِيسَـم (ĭsăm) *if I am*, اِيسَـك (ĭsăñ) *if thou art*, اِيسَـه (ĭsé) *if he is*;
اِيسَـك (ĭsék) *if we are*, اِيسَـكِز (ĭsăñĭz) *if you are*, اِيسَـلَر
(ĭsélér) *if they are*.

Past Active Participle.

اِيمِش (ĭmĭsh) *who or which was*.

Verbal Noun Perfect.

اِيدِك (ĭdĭk) *the fact of having been*.

Gerund.

اِيكَن (ĭkén, *old* اِيكَان ĭkăn) *during the fact of being*.

These fragments are made negative by prefixing the adverb
دِيكِل (dĭyĭl) *not*. Thus, دِيكِلِم (dĭyĭlĭm) *I am not*,
(dĭyĭl ĭdĭm) *I was not*; دِيكِل اِيسَـم (dĭyĭl ĭsém) *if I am not*;
دِيكِل اِيدِك (dĭyĭl ĭdĭk) not used as a verbal noun, but replaced
by اولْمَدِق (ŏlmădĭq) the negative verbal noun perfect of اولْمَق;
دِيكِل اِيكَن (dĭyĭl ĭkén) *while not being*.

The present tense indicative of the foregoing fragmentary
verb is completed, as to its third persons, singular and plural,

L

by using, when necessary only, the special, unique, and most distinctive Turkish invariable particle of affirmation, دِر (dĭr, dĭr) *is*, and its conventional (unnecessary) plural, دِرْلَرْ (dĭrlĕr, dĭrlăr) *are* (which is just as well expressed by the singular).

This word دِر, written in eastern Turkish دُور (dŭr), as it is still pronounced in provincial Ottoman, is often found also, in old and eastern writings, under the uncontracted form of دُورُورْ (dŭrŭr). This circumstance leads to a suspicion that the word is, originally, the aorist of the ordinary verb دُورْمَقْ (dŭrmăq) *to remain*.

However that may be, the peculiarity of the word is that it is not special to the third person singular, or to the two third persons, singular and plural. It is often used, in writing and in conversation, after a verb of the first or second person also, singular or plural, of any simple tense of the indicative, with or without the plural sign لَر, when the sense admits it. It is, in fact, an exact equivalent to the French inchoative expression *c'est que*, and the Latin *constat quod*, which can be used to introduce any indicative proposition, as the Turkish دِر is used to conclude and complete any such. And, as the French and Latin clauses can be omitted without the sense suffering, so also can the Turkish دِر. In conversation it is much more dispensed with than used.

The negative of دِر is دِر دِكِلْ (dĭr dĭl) *is not*; pl. دِكِلْلَرْ دِر

(dĭyĭllĕr dĭr) and ديكِلْ دِرْلَرْ (dĭyĭl dĭrlĕr) *are not* (just as well expressed without the لَرْ).

Section XIX. *The Verb of Presence and Absence, of Existence and Non-Existence.*

There are no such verbs in Turkish. What there are, and what Europeans have erroneously chosen to designate as such, are two *adjectives,* وَارْ (vår) *present* or *existent,* يُوقْ (yók) *absent* or *non-existent.* Like any other substantive or adjective, these may be followed by the verbal particle of affirmation دِرْ, which, in this case, as in any other case, may be omitted in conversation.

It may be convenient, occasionally, for a novice in Turkish to suppose that وَارْ or وَارْ دِرْ means *there is;* that يُوقْ or يُوقْ دُرْ means *there is not.* But, unless rightly understood, those renderings are misleading. The expressions really say and mean *he, she,* or *it, is present* (or *existent*); *he, she,* or *it, is absent* (or *non-existent*) ; as, آتَشْ وَارْ (åtĕsh vår) *fire* (is) *present* (here), or *existent* (somewhere); آتَشْ يُوقْ (åtĕsh yók) *fire* (is) *absent* (here), or *non-existent* (anywhere).

Then, such a phrase as وَارْ أُولْ (vår ól) *be thou present* (or *existent*), يُوقْ أُولْ (yók ól) *be thou absent* (or *non-existent*), becomes clear. The first is a kind of prayer, *Mayest thou ever exist, and be at hand, ready to help the afflicted!* while the

second is a condemnation, a sentence of banishment or
annihilation, or a wish in the nature of a curse, *Away!
Avaunt!* &c.

By using a locative with these two expressions, they become
special instead of general : جَيْبِمْدَه پَارَه وَار (jéblindá párá vár)
in my pocket money is present (I have some money in my
pocket) ; اَوِبمْدَه اُوطُونُمْ يُوقْ اِيدِى (évlmdé ódúnúm yóq ídl) *in my
house my firewood was absent, wanting, non-existent* (I had no
firewood in my house).

By using a possessive pronoun (with or without a genitive
as well) with these two expressions, the idea of possession is
superadded ; as, پَارَمْ وَار (párám vár) *money belonging to me
exists* (i. e., *I have money, I have some money*) ; پَارَكْ يُوقْ (párán
yóq) *money belonging to thee* (is) *non-existent* (i. e., *thou hast no
money*) ; بَابَاسِنك چُوقْ كِتَابْلَرِى وَارْدِر (bábá-lnlñ chóq kltáblárl vár
dlr) *many books belonging to his father are existent* (i. e., *his
father has many books*) ; بَنِمْ سَكَا اِحْتِيَاجِمْ يُوقْ اِيدِى (bénlm sáñá
lhtlyájlm yóq ídl) *any need of mine to* (lean on) *thee* (for assist-
ance) *was non-existent* (i. e., *I had no need of thee*).

SECTION XX.   *Of the Compound Verbs.*

Besides the Turkish verbs already described, the Ottoman
language has been indefinitely enriched with whole classes of

compound verbs, active and passive, transitive and intransitive, formed by a Turkish auxiliary verb preceded by a substantive or adjective of Arabic or Persian, even of foreign, origin.

An active compound verb is formed, generally, by an Arabic, rarely by a Persian verbal noun, or by a foreign substantive, followed by one of the auxiliaries ایتْمَكْ (ìtmèk, *vulg.* ètmèk), اَیْلَمَكْ (èylèmèk), قِلْمَقْ (qìlmâq) *to do,* or بُیُورْمَقْ (bùyùrmâq) *to command, to deign to do;* or by an Arabic (very seldom, a Persian, never a foreign) active participle, followed by the auxiliary اُولْمَقْ (òlmâq) *to be.* These verbs are either transitive or intransitive. The first three auxiliaries are identical in sense; the first is the most frequently used; the second often, the third occasionally, replaces it, so as to avoid repetition; and the fourth is used when a deferential tone is assumed in speaking or writing to or of a superior, and politely to or of an equal. Thus, اِرْسَالْ بُیُورْمَقْ اِرْسَالْ ایتْمَكْ (ìrsâl ètmèk) *to send;* (ìrsâl bùyùrmâq) *to deign or condescend to send, to favour by sending, to have the goodness to send;* مُوجِبْ اُولْمَقْ (mùjìb òlmâq) *to cause;* تَوَطُّنْ اَیْلَمَكْ (tèvâttùn èylèmèk) *to settle* (in a place, as a home); بَشِیمَانْ اُولْمَقْ (pèshīmān òlmâq) *to be regretfully or penitently sorry* (for some act); وِزِیتَه اِتْمَكْ (vìzìtè ètmèk) *to visit, to pay a visit.*

Transitive verbs of this class form their passives with the auxiliary اُولُنْمَقْ (òlùnmâq), which, by itself, does not admit of translation. Thus, ارْسَال اُوْلُنْمَق (Irsāl ôlûnmâq) *to be sent, to have done* (to it) *the action of being sent* (for the Arabic and Persian verbal nouns, the reverse of the more general Turkish rule, take the passive as well as the active sense). Deferential compound passives are formed with the passive auxiliary بُيُورُلْمَق (bûyûrûlmâq) ; as, ارْسَال بُيُورُلْمَق (Irsāl bûyûrûlmâq) *to be condescendingly sent, to be kindly sent.*

Reciprocal verbs active of this class are formed with the reciprocal of ايتْمَك, that is, with the auxiliary ايدِشْمَك (Idîsh-mêk) ; as, خُصُومَتْ ايدِشْمَك (khûsūmêt Idîshmêk) *mutually to exercise hostility, litigation, or spite, towards one another.*

Causatives of the simple and reciprocal are formed by the causatives of ايتْمَك and ايدِشْمَك, namely, ايتْدِرْمَك, ايدِشْدِرْمَك ; thus, خُصُومَتْ ايدِشْدِرْمَك ارْسَال ايتْدِرْمَك *to cause* or *let* (a thing) *be sent* ; *to cause* or *let* (two or more) *mutually attack each other.*

Negatives and impotentials, as also dubitatives, potentials, and faciles, are constructed with those forms of ايتْمَك and the other auxiliaries. Thus, ارْسَال ايدَهمَامَك *not to send* ; ارْسَال ايتْمَامَك *not to be able to send* ; ارْسَال ايتْمِشْ *it is said that he sent* ; ارْسَال ايدِيُورْمَك *to be able to send* ; ارْسَال ايدَه بِلْمَك *just to send.*

SECTION XXI. *Of the Interrogative Verb, and Interrogation in general.*

All interrogations, in Turkish (when an interrogative pronoun is not present in the phrase, as such), are made by introducing the interrogative particle or adverb مى (mi, mï) into its proper position in the phrase.

The proper position of this particle in the phrase is the end of the word on which the question turns. We have no equivalent for it in English; in Latin the word *an*, and the enclitic particle *ne*, are its equivalents; also the French *est-ce que?*

This may be best shown by an example of five elements, each of which may be the word on which the question specially turns, so that the adverb مى is successively joined to each of them to indicate that speciality. Thus:

1. سَنْمِى صَبَاحْ بَنِمْلَه عَرَبَيَه بِنَهجَكسِينْ (sånmi såbāh bènimlå 'årå-båyå binèjèksin)

Is it *thou* who art to ride with me to-morrow in the carriage?

2. سَنْ صَبَاحْمِى بَنِمْلَه عَرَبَيَه بِنَهجَكسِينْ (sån såbāhmi bènimlå 'årå-båyå bènèjèksin)

Is it *to-morrow* that thou art to ride with me in the carriage?

3. سَنْ صَبَاحْ بَنِمْلَامِى عَرَبَيَه بِنَهجَكسِينْ (sån såbāh bènimlåmi 'årå-båyå binèjèksin)

Is it with *me* that thou art to ride in the carriage to-morrow?

4. سَنْ صَبَاحْ بَنْمْلَه عَرَبَيَمِى بِنَجَكْسِين (sån såbāh bėnĭmlå 'åråbayå-
mĭ bĭnėjėksĭn)

Is it *in the carriage* that thou art to ride with me to-morrow?

5. سَنْ صَبَاحْ بَنْمْلَه عَرَبَيَه بِنَجَكْمِيسِين (sån såbāh bėnĭmlå 'åråbåyå
bĭnėjėkmĭsĭn)

Art thou *going to ride* with me to-morrow in the carriage?

This does not, however, exhaust the possible points of the
question in the case of this sentence, nor the proper places of
the adverb مِى in it. The phrase itself may be in question, as
to whether these words were used, or some others, by the
person to whom the interrogation is addressed. In that case,
the adverb مِى would stand after the personal ending of the
verb; سَنْ صَبَاحْ بَنْمْلَه عَرَبَيَه بِنَجَكْسِين مِى (sån såbāh bėnĭmlå 'årå-
båyå bĭnėjėksĭn mĭ), which means, *Dost thou say, thou wilt ride
with me to-morrow in the carriage?*

The last two instances call specially for the explanation that,
in compound verbs the proper place of the adverb مِى may be
between the two elements of the verb. Thus we may ask,
إِرْسَالْ مِى اِيدَجَكْ *Is it* to send (and not himself *carry*, for instance)
that he is going to do? and إِرْسَالْ اِيدَجَكْمِى (ĭrsāl ĭdėjėkmĭ)
Is he going to send?

In Turkish simple or derivative verbs, supposing that the
adverb مِى is to follow the verb in the sentence, and not some

other member thereof, then a further question is seen to arise
in No. 5 above given, as to the exact part of the verb itself
that takes this word after it. In this respect, the tenses have
first to be considered. The simple tenses take the adverb at
the end of the tense-root, and their compounds also, before
their auxiliary ايدِى ; thus, ايدِيُورْمِى *is he doing?* ايدِيُورْمِى ايدِى
was he doing? Next, a distinction has to be made between
the third persons, singular and plural, as one group, and the
first and second persons, singular and plural also, as another
group. The first-named group of tenses have no personal
endings, the second group have special personal endings, and
the interrogative precedes these, following the tense-root still;
thus, تَپِيُورْمِيِمْ (tèpìyòrmìyìm) *am I kicking?* تَپِيُورْمِيسِين (tèpìyòr-
mìsìn) *art thou kicking?* تَپِيُورْمِى (tèpìyòrmì) *is he kicking?*
تَپِيُورْمِييِزْ (tèpìyòrmìyìz) *are we kicking?* تَپِيُورْمِيسِكِنْزْ (tèpìyòr-
mìsìnìz) *are you kicking?* تَپِيُورْلَرْمِى (tèpìyòrlèrmì) *are they
kicking?*

The perfect tense indicative forms an exception to the foregoing rule, as it takes the interrogative after the personal
endings. Thus, تَپْدِمْمِى (tèpdìmmì) *have I kicked? did I kick?*
تَپْدِيمِى (tèpdìñmì) *hast thou kicked? didst thou kick?*
(tèpdìmì) *has he kicked? did he kick?* تَپْدِكْمِى (tèpdìkmì)
have we kicked? did we kick? تَپْدِيكِنْزْمِى (tèpdìñìzmì) *have you
kicked? did you kick?* تَپْدِيلَرْمِى (tèpdìlèrmì) *have they kicked?
did they kick?*

SECTION XXII. *Of Adverbial Expressions.*

As explained in Section II., every Turkish adjective is also
an adverb.

Every noun of time is also used as an adverb; as, صَبَاح كَلْ
(sâbâh gâl) *come to-morrow;* أَرْكَنْ كَلْدِى (érkén gâldî) *he came
early;* أَخْشَامْ كَلُورْ (âkhshâm gélîr) *he will come in the evening.*

Adjectives of relative place, like all adjectives, are used as
adverbs; thus, يُوقَارِى چِيق (yúqârî chîq) *mount up, walk up,
climb up, ascend;* أَشَاغِى كَلْ (âshâghî gâl) *come down, descend;*
ايلَرُو كِيتْ (îlérî gît) *go forward, advance;* كَيرُوكَلْ (gérî gâl)
come back.

But substantives of place, like all substantives, can be used
adverbially by the sole means of being joined to prepositions;
thus, يُوقَارِيدَه اُوتُورِيُورْ (yúqârîdâ ótûrîyór) *he is sitting higher up;*
أَشَاغِيدَنْ كَلِيُورُمْ (âshâghîdân gélîyórîm) *I am coming from below;*
صَاغَه كِيتْ (sâghâ gît) *go to the right;* &c.

A possessive pronoun may enter into such an adverbial
expression; as, اُوسْتُمَه چِيقْدِى (ústûmâ chîqdî) *he mounted on to
the top of me.*

An adjective, substantive, and preposition may join to form
an adverbial expression; as, آلْتْ طَرَفْدَه (âlt târâfdâ) *on the lower
side, lower down;* آلْتْ طَرَفْدَنْ (âlt târâfdân) *from the lower side;
from lower down.*

So an adjective, substantive, possessive, and preposition may
be combined in an adverbial expression ; as, أُرْسْتْ يَانَمِه (ûst
yánîmå) *to the side above me ;* آلَتْ يَانِكَدَ (ált yánîñdá) *on the
side below thee ;* صَاغْ طَرَفِنْدَنْ (ságh táráfîndán) *from his (her, its)
right-hand side.*

With certain special exceptions, any Arabic substantive or
adjective becomes an adverb by adding an ûstûn and vowel ا
to it ; this being often marked with a double ûstûn sign, and
read án ; or, if the word is a feminine in ة, by putting two
dots, with or without the double ûstûn sign to it, without
an ا ; thus, طُولًا (tûlán) *in length, longwise, in longitude ;*
عَرْضًا ('árzán) *in breadth, breadthwise, in latitude ;* بَرًّا وَ بَحْرًا
(bérrán ûé báhrán) *by land and by sea ;* مُقَدَّمًا (múqáddémá)
formerly ; مُوَخَّرًا mú'ákhkhárán) *latterly, recently ;* قَطْعًا وَ قَاطِبَةً
(qát'án vé qátîbétán) *decidedly and entirely.*

The first ten Arabic ordinals are thus much used adver-
bially ; as, أَوَّلًا (ávválá) *firstly;* ثَانِيًا (sániyá) *secondly ;* ثَالِثًا (sálisá)
thirdly ; رَابِعًا (rúbî'á) *fourthly ;* خَامِسًا (khámîsá) *fifthly ;* سَادِسًا
(sádisá) *sixthly ;* سَابِعًا (sábî'á) *seventhly ;* ثَامِنًا (sámîné) *eighthly ;*
تَاسِعًا (tásî'á) *ninthly ;* عَاشِرًا ('áshîrá) *tenthly.*

Section XXIII. *Of Prepositions.*

They always follow the substantive or pronoun. Besides those given in the chapter on the substantive, there are but four or five others : اوزَرَه (üzèrè) *upon,* جَ (jè, jà) *according to,* سِزْ (sìz) and سِزِين (sìzìn) *without,* لَین (lèyìn) *at the time of, after the manner of.*

Section XXIV. *Of Conjunctions.*

The conjunctions دَ (dà) and دَخِی (dàkhì) *also,* follow the word they unite to a preceding one ; as, كِیدَرْسَكْ بَنْدَه كِیدَرِمْ (gìdèrsàn, bèn-dà gìdèrìm) *if thou wilt go, I also will go ;* بُو دَخِی (bù dàkhì) *this, too.*

All other conjunctions head the clauses which they connect.

The principal of these are : وَ (vè, in Persian couplets read û, û) *and ;* اَمَّا (àmmà), لَكِنْ (làkìn), وَلَكِنْ (vè-làkìn) *but ;* اَنْجَقْ (ànjàq) *only ;* اَكَرْ (èyèr, ègèr) *if ;* یَاخُودْ (yàkhòd) *or ;* ...یَا ...یَا (yà... yà...) *either... or...;* ...نَه ...نَه (nè... nè...) *neither... nor...;* حَتَّی (hàttà) *insomuch that ;* مَكَرْ (mèyèr, mègèr) *unless ;* اِمْدِی (ìmdì) *therefore, wherefore ;* زِیرَا (zìrà) *for, because ;* چُونْکه (chûnkû) *since, by reason that ;* که (kì) *that ;* تَا (tà) *so that, in order that ; as far as.* Of these, some are Turkish, some Arabic, others Persian in origin.

SECTION XXV. *Of Interjections.*

These are mostly Arabic or Persian in origin. They pre-cede, as in English. The principal are : اَیْ (éy), یَا (yā) *O ;* آهْ (āh) *ah ;* اَیْوَاهْ (éywāh) *alas ;* خَیْفْ (kháyf) *woe ;* مَدَدْ (médéd) *help ;* آفَرِینْ (āférīn, *vulg.* āférīm) *bravo.*

There is, however, a peculiar Turkish interjection آ (á) *O,* that joins on to the vocative following it ; as, آبَابَا (á-bábá) *O father ;* آاَنَا (á-ǎnǎ) *O mother.* It also follows nouns, pronouns, and verbs, taking the sense of *Yes ! Indeed ! I told you so ! You see now !* as, آدَمَا (ádǎm-á) *a man ; you see !* کُوزَلْ (gyúzél-á) *nice ; indeed !* بَنِمَا (bénĭm-á) *mine ; in sooth !* کُورَمَدِکَا (gyúrémá-diñ-á) *thou couldst not see ; after all !*

CHAPTER III.

THE OTTOMAN SYNTAX.

SECTION I. *Conversational brevity. Precision in writing.*

COLLOQUIAL and written Ottoman Turkish, as far as Syntax is concerned, are the very antipodes of each other.

As in the orthography the rule is given : " Never introduce a vowel-letter into a Turkish or foreign word without removing a possible doubt as to pronunciation ; never leave out a vowel in such a word, if by the omission a doubt is created as to pronunciation,"—that is, be always as concise as is possible without falling into ambiguity ; so also, in colloquial syntax the chief rule is : *Never repeat a word, or introduce its equivalent, and never use a subsidiary word, unless for the sake of emphasis;* whereas the golden rule for written language is, *Never omit any word that tends to make a sentence clear and explicit. On the contrary, introduce freely as many new words as may, in the requisite degree, elucidate the sense sought to be conveyed.* In other words, *Spoken Ottoman Turkish should be as concise as possible, even to the verge of ambiguity;*

written Ottoman Turkish must be as full, verbally, as to leave no doubt on the mind of the reader at any distance of space or time. The reasons are obvious and eminently practical, philosophical; namely: If, by reason of a speaker's conciseness, a doubt as to his meaning should arise in the mind of the person addressed, a question can be put, and the doubt at once removed; if, on the contrary, a written document be left obscure in any part, the doubt thence arising must remain unsolved, and the meaning guessed at, because the writer is either dead or away at a distance.

Hence, if one be asked, بُو نَه دِر (bù nè dìr) *what is this?* the answer, in Ottoman Turkish, will be, for instance, اَلْمَا (èlmà) *an apple,* as in English. (A Frenchman would answer: *"C'est une pomme."*) Should the question be, قَرِنْدَاشِمِى كُورْدِيـكُـزْمِى (qàrndàshìmì [*vulg.* qàrdàshìmì] gyùrdùnùz-mù) *have you seen my brother?* the answer will be, either كُورْدُمْ (gyùrdùm) *I have seen* (him), or كُـورْمَـدِمْ (gyùrmàdìm) *I have not seen* (him). Should one say to you, بُونِى سَكَا وِرْسَمْ يَرمِيسِينْ (bùnù sànà vèrsàm, yèr-mì-sìn) *If I give this to thee* (you), *wilt thou* (will you) *eat* (it)? the answer will be either يَرِمْ (yèrìm) *I will eat* (it), or يَمَامْ (yèmàm) *I will not eat* (it). In this last question, the omission of " it," even by the asker, is to be remarked.

As instances of the omission of all possible subsidiary words from phrases in conversation, may be mentioned that of the

affirmative در (dir) *is, it is, he* or *she is*, on all occasions of
ordinary assertion or negation. The personal and corroborative possessive pronouns are never employed in conversation
unless for emphasis or distinction ; as, سَوِيُورِم (séviyórìm) *I
love* (thee, you, him, her, it), سَنِي سَوِيُورِم (sáni séviyórìm) *I love
thee* (you), بَنْ سَنِي سَوِيُورِم (bén sáni ...) *I, personally, love thee ;*
بَابَام كَلْدِى (bábàm gáldì) *my father came,* or *has come.*

As a consequence of the desire to leave no doubt as to the
meaning of a writing, nouns and verbs in apposition, in pairs,
are much used ; such are, وِدّ وَمَحَبَّت (vidd ù máhàbbèt) *friend-
ship,* تَحْرِيرُ وَنَسْطِيرْ اُولُنْدُى (táhrīr ù tàstīr ólùndù) *has been written.*

A result of the avoidance of unnecessary repetition is that
the third person singular of a verb is often employed instead
of its plural when the nominative plural is expressed ; as,
آدَمْلَرْ كَلْدِى (ádàmlàr gáldì) *some men,* or *the men have come,* or
came.

Another such result is the use of a singular substantive with
a plural cardinal number ; as, اُوچْ آتْ (úch át) *three horses,*
بِيكْ عَرَبَه (bĩñ 'áràbà) *a thousand vehicles* (carriages, carts,
waggons, &c.).

To make written composition still more precise, it is very
usual, after introducing a common substantive or a proper
name into a paragraph or article, letter, dispatch, &c., never
to use a personal pronoun to designate the thing or person

so named, but to repeat the substantive or proper name as often as may be required, either preceded or followed by one of the indicative adjectives, مَزْبُور (mézbūr), مَذْكُور (mézkyūr), for things or persons, مَسْفُور (mésfūr), for a contemned or criminal person, مُومَى اِلَيْه (mūmá iléy-h), for a reputable person, and مُشَارٌ اِلَيْه (múshārún iléy-h), for a person of rank and consideration. These words all mean, in reality, *the aforesaid, the afore-mentioned, the said,* &c. In the case of a *person* first mentioned by name, or by a common substantive, these words may be used as substantives,—we might say,—as a kind of personal or demonstrative pronoun, in all the cases of the declension; but, in the case of a *thing*, they must be used as adjectives to its name, repeated each time.

SECTION II. *Syntax of the Substantive.*

A common noun substantive singular may be either definite or indefinite, and may represent, according to circumstances or the context, either an individual or the individual, several individuals, a portion of the species, or the whole species; as,

بَاغْچَه كُوزَل شَیْ (bághchá gyúzél shéy) *a garden* (is) *a pretty thing;*

پَادِشَاهْ كَلْدِی (pādishāh gáldi) *the monarch came,* or *has come;*

اِنْكِلْتَرَهدَه كَمِی جُوق (îngîltérádá gémi chóq) *in England* (there are)

many ships ; جیچک باغچەنک زینتی در (chichèk bâghchânïñ zïnètï
dïr) *flowers are the ornaments of the gardens, of the garden* ;
صو ایچدم (sù ïchdïm) *I drank* (some) *water, I drank water* (not
wine, &c.), صو آقار (sù âqâr) *water flows.*

In the accusative case indefinite, the substantive is as in the
nominative ; as, صو ایچمك (sù ïchmèk) *to drink water* (some
water). If the declensional accusative is used, it is always
definite ; as, صویی ایچدم (sùyù ïchdïm) *I drank*, or *have drunk*,
the *water.*

There are four different Turkish methods of constructing
two substantives in a sentence. First, by simple juxtaposition ;
second, by adding the possessive suffix of the third person to
the second substantive ; third, by putting the first in the
genitive, and still adding the possessive suffix to the second ;
and fourth, by putting the first in some other prepositional
case, and leaving the second unchanged.

In simple juxtaposition of two substantives, the first indicates a material, the second a form ; or, the first indicates a
quantity, the second a material ; as, آلتون قوطی (âltïn qùtù) *a
gold box* ; بر کیله آرپه (bïr kïlè ârpâ) *a bushel* (of) *barley* ;
ایکی ساعتلك یول (ïkï sā'âtlïk yòl) *a distance of two hours journey* ;
اوچ ستریلك چوخه (ùch sètrïlïk chòhâ) *broadcloth enough for three*
coats.

With the possessive suffix alone added, a relation of genus and species is indicated, the genus standing last, and the combination remaining indefinite; as, كِتَابْ قَابِى (kltāb qâbî) *a book-cover*; اَوْ كُوپَكِى (êv kyûpèyî) *a house (domestic) dog*; يَبَانْ اُرْدَكِى (yâbân ûrdèyî) *a duck of the wilderness (wild duck)*. If the first is a proper name, the second is the species, the first the name of the individual, and the combination is definite; as, آزَاقْ دَكِزِى (âzâq dèñîzî) *the Sea of Azof*.

With the first in the genitive, real possession is indicated, the name of the possessor being the first, and the combination is definite; as, قِرَالِكْ عَسْكَرِى (qîrālîñ 'áskêrî) *the king's army*; بَابَامِكْ اَوِى (bâbâmîñ èvî) *my father's house*.

When the first is put into a prepositional case, the second remains without a suffix, and the combination may be definite or indefinite, an active participle being always understood; as, شَهْرَهْ يُولْ (shèhrè yòl) *a (or the) road to the town*; دَمِرْدَنْ كُوپْرِى (dèmîrdân kyûprû) *a bridge of iron*; آيَدَهْ بِرْ كَرَّهْ (âydâ blr kèrrè) *once in a month*; &c.

When two substantives are in apposition, no change is made in either; as, چَاوُشْ آغَا (châwûsh âghâ) *Mr. Sergeant*; يَازِيجِى اَفَنْدِى (yâzljl èfèndl) *Mr. Clerk*; مُشِيرْ پَاشَا (mûshīr pâshâ) *the Pasha (who is) a Mushir*. Here, the generic word stands last, and the combination is definite. Sometimes, the specific word or term is complex and obeys its own rules; as, أُونْ بَاشِى آغَا (ŏn-bâshî âghâ) *Mr. Corporal*; مِيرْ آلَاىْ بَكْ (mīr-âlāy bèy) *Squire Colonel*; مِـيـرِ لِوَا بَاشَا (mīrl-līvā pâshâ) *the Major-General Pasha.*

There are two exceptions to the rule that the generic word stands last, when the other word is a proper name. In all other cases with proper names, this rule holds good; as, أَسْمَا سُلْطَانْ (èsmā sûltān) *Princess Esma,* عِزَّتْ مُوَلَّا (ìzzèt mŏllâ) *Judge Izzet;* عَارِفْ اَفَنْدِى ('ārif èfèndî) *Mr. 'Arif;* &c. The exceptions are: 1, the word سُلْطَانْ, when applied to the sovereign before his name; as, سُلْطَانْ عَبْدُ الْحَمِيد (sûltān 'âbdû-'l-hâmîd); 2, the word مُوَلَّا, when applied to a student or schoolboy, also before his name; as, مُوَلَّا رَاشِـد (mŏllâ rāshîd) *schoolboy Rashid.*

Any number of substantives may be in apposition, and one of them may be the proper name of the individual; as, أُوغْـلُمْ قُولُكُزْ (ŏghlûm qûlûñûz) *your servant, my son;* أُوغْلُمْ رَفِيقْ بَكْ قُولُكُزْ (ŏghlûm rèfîq bèy qûlûñûz) *your servant, my son, Refiq Bey;* أُوغْـلُمْ مِيرْ آلَاىْ رَفِيقْ بَكْ قُولُكُـزْ (ŏghlûm mīr-âlāy rèfîq bèy qûlûñûz) *your servant, my son, Colonel Refiq Bey;* &c.

When a string of substantives in construction would in strictness require several of them consecutively to be put in the genitive case, the monotonous cacophony of the repetition of the preposition is avoided by omitting it once or twice where most appropriate; thus, آتِی اُوغْلُنُكْ دَایِیسِنِكْ اَنِشْتَهسِنِكْ پَاشَانِكْ (pàshànìñ ènìshtèsìnìñ dàyìsìnìñ óghlùnùñ àtì) *the horse of the son of the uncle of the brother-in-law of the pasha*, may be expressed in either of the following ways: پَاشَانِكْ اَنِشْتَهسِی دَایِیسِی or بَاشَا اَنِشْتَهسِنِكْ دَایِیسِی اُوغْلُنُكْ آتِی, or اُوغْلُنُكْ آتِی or بَاشَا اَنِشْتَهسِی; the last پَاشَانِكْ اَنِشْتَهسِی دَایِیسِنِكْ اُوغْلُنُكْ آتِی, or دَایِیسِنِكْ اُوغْلُنُكْ آتِی; the last genitive preposition being, perhaps, the most frequently retained and necessary.

Two or more Arabic or Persian substantives may be put in Persian construction with each other. Their order is then the reverse of what it would be in Turkish construction, just as in English *the king's horse* is in reverse order with *the horse of the king*. In Persian construction each preceding substantive of a series must be *vocally* connected with its consequent. This *vocal connexion* is effected by making the final quiescent consonant of the preceding substantive movent with èsèrè; thus, شَاهْ فَرْمَانِ (fèrmànì shàh) *the command of the king*; مَضْمُونِ فَرْمَانِ شَاهِ اِیرَانْ (mùzmùnù fèrmànì shàhì ìràn) *the tenour of the command of the king of Persia*. But, if the last consonant of a preceding substantive is movent, and followed by a vowel-letter, a servile consonant must be introduced to support the èsèrè vowel of connexion; and this consonant varies with the final vowel of the word. When the final vowel-letter is ‌ا‌ or ‌و‌, the servile consonant is ‌ی‌; as, جَای پَای اَسْپ (jā-yĭ pā-yĭ èsb) *the place of the foot of the horse*; مُوی رُوی سَگ (mū-yŭ rū-yu sèg) *the hair of the face of the dog*. If the final vowel-letter be a ‌ی‌, this letter is converted itself into the servile consonant required; so that no written addition is needed; thus, پَرِی جَاهِ بُرْج (pèrī-yĭ chāh-ĭ bŭrj) *the fairy of the well of the tower*. Ignorance often writes a hèmzè over such final ‌ی‌ so converted into a consonant; but it really is not requisite. If, however, the final vowel be the letter ‌ه‌, then the addition of a hèmzè is a necessity. Sometimes the èsèrè vowel-sign is figured under it, ‌هٍ‌. Usage is divided as to the proper place where the servile hèmzè should be written. It is at times more correctly placed between the two words, on a line with the writing; as, بَرَهِ فَلَک (bèrè-ĭ fèlèk) *the lamb of the sphere* (i.e., Aries); and otherwise it is less correctly placed over the vowel ‌ه‌; as بَرَهٔ فَلَک.

Of two substantives in Persian construction, the first is often the metaphorical name of the thing literally expressed by the second, the pair really representing one idea under two images; as, سَائِقِ تَقْدِیر (sāĭqĭ tèqdīr) *the drover, destiny*; عِنَانِ عَزِیمَت ('ĭnānĭ 'àzīmèt) *the reins* (of) *departure*.

Whether in Turkish or Persian construction, the same remark holds good of a pair of substantives, one of which is

the word اَمْر (émr), or one of its synonyms, مَادَّه (māddé),
خُصُوص (khúsūs), كَيْفِيَّتْ (kéyflyyét), &c., all of which signify
our *circumstance,* and the like. They are used in written
Turkish for precision. Thus: رَاهِ تَحْصِيلِكْ اَمْرِ انْسِلَاكِى (rāh-ı tảh-
sīlīn émr-ı ínsílākí) *the matter of the pursuit of the path of
study;* دُونَانْمَدِنِكْ كَلْمَسِى خُصُوصُى (dónảnmảnīn gélmésí khúsūsú)
the question of the coming of the fleet.

After a proper name of a person or thing, the word نَامْ (nām)
name, is commonly employed; as, اَحْمَدْ نَامْ ذَاتْ (ảhméd nām zāt)
the personage named Ahmed; قِرِيمْ نَامْ جَزِيرَه (qírím nām jézīré)
the island (peninsula) *named Crimea.*

The two words حَضْرَتْ (hảzrét), جَنَابْ (jénāb), which
originally mean *presence* and *side,* are used before or after the
names or titles of individuals held in honour, with a meaning
varying from that of *His Divine Majesty* down to that of plain
Mr. or *Mrs.,* &c. When they precede, they remain unchanged
to the eye, but are in Persian construction; as, حَضْرَتِ خُدَا
(hảzrét-ı khúdā) *His Divine Majesty, God;* حَضْرَتِ پَيْغَمْبَرْ
(— péygảmbér) *His Sanctity, the Prophet;* جَنَابْ پَادِشَاهْ
(jénāb-ı pādíshāh) *His Majesty, the Sovereign;* جَنَابِ صَدَارَتْمَآبْ
(— sảdārét-mả·āb) *His Highness, the Repair of the Vezirate*
(the Grand Vezir). When they follow, they are in Turkish
construction, and generally take the possessive pronominal

suffix of the third person plural, but sometimes that of the third person singular; as, شَيْخُ الْإِسْلَامْ طَاهِرْ بَكْ حَضْرَتْلَرِى (sheykhú-'l-islām tāhir bey hǎzrět.ěrǐ) *His Eminence the Lord High Chancellor, Tahir Bey;* بُرُوسَه مُفْتِيسِى حَسَنْ افَنْدِى جَنَابِى (bǔrūsǎ mǔftǐsǐ hǎsǎn ěfěndǐ jěnābǐ) *His Honour the State Counsel of Brusa, Hasan Efendi;* سَفِيرْ پَاشَا حَضْرَتْلَرِى (sěfīr pǎshǎ —) *His Excellency the Pasha Ambassador;* تَرْجُمَانْ بَكْ جَنَابْلَرِى (těrjǔmān bey —) *His Worship the Interpreter Bey;* &c., &c., &c. Generally, the word حَضْرَتْ before a single name indicates one of the prophets, saints, or patriarchs of old; as, حَضْرَتِ نُوحْ (hǎzrětǐ nūh) *the patriarch Noah;* مُوسَى — (— mūsǎ) *the prophet Moses;* سُلَيْمَانْ — (— sǔlěymān) *the prophet* (king) *Solomon;* مَرْيَمْ — (— měryěm) *Saint Mary* (the Virgin Mother); عِيسَى — (— 'īsǎ) *the Prophet Jesus;* مَسِيحْ — (— měsīh) *the holy Anointed One* (Christ); &c., &c., &c.

SECTION III. *Syntax of the Adjective.*

Nearly everything requisite in a sketch has been said on this subject in the former Chapter (II.), Section II. If several adjectives qualify one substantive, they follow one another simply in Turkish construction, and are all connected vocally in the Persian construction; as, كُوزَلْ ادِبْلُو مَحْجُوبْ چُوجُقْ (gyǔzěl, édèbli, mâhjūb chòjùq) *a pretty, well-behaved, modest child;*

جَای بِهِشْت نُمَای فَرَحْ فَـزَا (jā-yi blhlsht-nûmā-yi fèrâh-fèzā) *a paradise-like, joy-giving place.*

One adjective may qualify several substantives in a sentence; as, أَمَمُ وَأَجْيَالٍ سَائِرَه (ûmèm ù èjyāli sâʾlrè) *the other peoples and nations.*

An Arabic or Persian adjective is never placed *after* a Turkish or foreign substantive; and whenever either is placed *before* one of these, it remains, like a Turkish adjective, unchanged as to gender or number; as, عَظِيمْ طَاغ ('âzīm dâgh) *a great mountain;* عَظِيمْ پَادِشَاهْ ('âzīm pādlshāh) *a great monarch,* عَظِيمْ دَوْلَتْ ('âzīm dèvlèt) *a great state.*

Some adjectives take a substantive as a complement to restrict their application. In Turkish construction, this complement precedes, with or without a preposition; as, صُوطُولُو (sù dòlù) *full (of) water,* صُوایِلَه طُولُو (sù llâ dòlù) *filled with water.* In Persian construction it follows; as, لَایِقِ بَیَانْ (lāyiq-i bèyān) *worthy of exposition;* مُوَافِقِ طَبْع (mùwāflq-i tâb') *conformable with nature.*

The Turkish adjective كِبِی (glbl) *like,* follows substantives, the personal pronoun of the 3rd pers. plur., the demonstratives plural, the interrogatives singular and plural, and the compound relatives, when its complements, without any change occurring in them; as, صُوكِبِی (sù glbl) *like water;* آنْلَرکِبِی (ânlèr

gìbì) *like them ;* بُونْلَرْ کِبِی (bùnlår gìbì) *like these ;* کِيمْ کِبِی
(kìm gìbì) *like whom ?* نَلَرْ کِبِی (nèlèr gìbì) *like what things ?*
بَابَامِكْکِی کِبِی (båbåmìñkì gìbì) *like the one belonging to my*
father ; بَنْدَکِی کِبِی (bèndèkì gìbì) *like the one I have.* All
other pronouns are put in the genitive, when complements to
this word ; as, بَنِمْ کِبِی (bènìm gìbì) *like me ;* اَنِكْ کِبِی (ånìñ
gìbì) *like him, her, it ;* سِزِكْ کِبِی (sìzìñ gìbì) *like you ;* بُونُكْ کِبِی
(bùnùñ gìbì) *like this ;* &c.

SECTION IV. *Syntax of the Numerals.*

The Turkish and Persian cardinals always precede their
substantive, and this is usually left in the singular, whatever
the number ; as, اِیکِی جِفْت (ìkì chìft) *two pairs ;* دُو جِهَانْ (dù
jìhån) *the two worlds* (present and future). But the Arabic
cardinal follows, the construction is made Persian, and the
substantive is made plural ; as, قُوَای خَمْسَه (qùvåyì khåmsè) *the*
five senses ; جِهَاتِ سِتَّه (jìhåtì sìttè) *the six directions* (in space),
six sides (of a solid).

The Turkish and Persian numerals precede the adjectives of
the same substantive ; as do also the Arabic (though after the
substantive) ; thus, اِیکِی سِیَاهْ کَچِی (ìkì sìyåh kèchì) *two black*
goats ; هَفْتْ اِقْلِیم مَعْمُورَه (hèft ìqlìm-ì må'mùrè) *the seven climates*

of the habitable earth ; ظَاهِرَه خَمْسَهٔ قُوَاى (qùvàyì khâmsè-ì zū-hìrè) *the five external senses.*

But if, instead of an adjective, a descriptive phrase should qualify the substantive, the Turkish numeral comes between the two; as, بِرْايِپْ بُوِينْدَه اُوطَهنِكْ (òdànìñ bòyùndà bìr ìp) *a string of the length of the room;* هَرْبِرى بَشْ كَيْسَه آقْچَه اِيدَرْ يَدِى اَلْمَاسْ (hèr bìrì bèsh kèysè àqchà èdèr yèdì èlmàs) *seven diamonds, each of the value of five purses of money.*

A Turkish cardinal number can be placed after a substantive in the genitive, singular or plural. It does not then define the number of that substantive, but of a definite portion of what this represents ; as, بِرى آدَمِكْ (àdàmìñ bìrì) *one of mankind, a man;* آدَمْلَرِكْ بِرى (àdàmlèrìñ bìrì) *one of the men;* اُوطَهنِكْ اِيكِيسِى (òdànìñ ìkìsì) *two rooms,* اُوطَهلَرِكْ اِيكِيسِى (òdàlàrìn ìkìsì) *two of the rooms.*

Very often, between the Turkish cardinal number and its substantive, another substantive is introduced, with the sense of *individual* or *individuals,* as in our phrases "*ten head of cattle,*" "*six sail of ships,*" &c. This substantive varies in Turkish according to the nature of the things defined by the numeral. For *men* it is نَفَرْ (nèfèr) *individual;* for *beasts* it is رَأْسْ (rè's) *head;* for *bulbs* it is بَاشْ (bàsh) *head;* for *ships* it is قِطْعَه (qìt'à) *piece;* for *cannons, ships,* and *villages,* it is پَارَه (pūrè,

vulg. pårå) *piece;* for things *usually counted* it is عَدَدْ ('ådèd)
number; for things *not usually counted* it is دَانَه (dānè, *vulg.*
tānå) *berry;* for *swords* it is قَبْضَه (qåbzå) *hilt;* for *elephants,*
زَنْجِیر (zènjīr) *chain.*   Thus : بَشْ نَفَرْ اَدَمْ *five men;* اُونْ رَأْسْ قُویُونْ
ten sheep; ایکی بَاشْ صُوغَانْ *two onions;* یِکِرْمِی قِطْعَه سَفِینَه *twenty
ships;* بِکِرْمِی بَارَه طُوبْ *twenty vessels;* اُونْ بَارَه تَكْنَه *ten cannon*
(pieces of artillery); اَلَّی بَارَه كُویْ یُوزْ عَدَدْ یُومُورْطَه *fifty villages;*
a hundred eggs; ایکی دَانَه اِنْجُو *two pearls;* اُوچْ قَبْضَه قِلِیجْ *three*
swords; بِرْ زَنْجِیر فِیل *one elephant.*

The Turkish ordinals precede their substantives ; as, بِرِنْجِی كِیجَه
(bìrìnjì gèyjè) *the first night;* اَلْتْمِشْ طُقُوزُنْجُی آلَیْ (åltmìsh
dòqùzùnjù ālåy) *the sixty-ninth regiment.*

The Arabic ordinals follow ; as, بَاب خَامِسْ (bābì khāmìs)
chapter the fifth.

The Persian ordinals generally precede, but sometimes
follow.

The Turkish distributive numerals are used to express the
rates of collection as well as of distribution ; as, بَشَرْ بَارَه وِیرْدِیلَرْ
(bèshèr pårå vèrdìlèr) *they contributed five paras each;* آنْلَرَه بَشَرْ
بَارَه وِیرِلْدِی (ånlårå bèshèr pårå vèrìldì) *to them five paras each*
were distributed.

For emphasis sake, the simpler distributives are often

repeated; but they are then generally used as substantives; as,

بِرَرْ بِرَرْ طُوپْلادِمْ (bìrèr bìrèr tòpládìm) *I collected* (them) *one by one;*

اِيكِيشَرْ اِيكِيشَرْ آلِيڭِيز (ìkìshèr ìkìshèr álìñìz) *take ye* (them) *two apiece each* (of you), or, *take you* (or thou, them) *two together each time.*

Section V. *Syntax of Pronouns.*

The demonstrative pronoun, when an adjective, precedes all other qualifications of its substantive; as, بُو أُوچ بِيُوكْ كُوزَلْ (bù ùch bìyùk gyùzèl gèlìnlìk qìz) كَلِيڭْلِكْ قِيز *these three tall, handsome, nubile girls.*

The suffixed possessive pronoun is not, in literary style, necessarily attached to its substantive, but to the last word of the combination of substantive, adjective, &c., to which it belongs.   Thus, مَرْحُومْ پَدَرِمْ (mèrhùm pèdèrìm) *my late father,* may be rendered in the Persian form, پَدَرِ مَرْحُومُمْ (pèdèr-ì mèr- hùmùm); so also, وَجْهِ خَاطِرْخَواهِيمِزْ (vèjh-ì khātìr-kh'āhìmìz) *the manner desiderated in mind by us* (i. e., *by me*); اَقْطَارِ شَرْقِيَّه سَرْعَسْكَرِ ظَفَرْرَهْبَرِى (áqtār-ì shàrqìyyè sèr-'àskèr-ì zàfèr-rèhbèrì) *the victorious commander-in-chief of the eastern districts;* بُوباغِنْ هَرْ بِرْ جَاِى جَانْفَزَاِى بِهِشْتْ اِنْتِمَاسِى (bù bàghìñ hèr bìr jā-yì jān-fèzā-yì bìhìsht-ìntìmāsì) *each soul-enrapturing, paradise-prognosticating spot of this garden.*

The corroborative of the suffixed possessive pronoun of

Turkish construction precedes the whole combination to which the possessive is suffixed ; and this corroborative is always in the genitive, whether it be a substantive or a pronoun ; as, بِنِمْ مَرْحُومْ پَدَرِمْ (bènĭm mèrhūm pèdèrĭm) *my late father*; أُوطَدَنِكْ بِيُوكْ قَپُوسِى (ôdânĭñ bĭyûk qâpûsû) *the great door. of the room.*

One possessive suffix may qualify several substantives ; as, آلِ وَ أَصْحَابْ وَ عِتْرَتْ وَ أَحْبَابِى (āl û âs-hāb û 'ĭtrèt û âhbābî) *his family, companions, posterity, and friends.*

SECTION VI.   *Syntax of the Verb.*

Verbs of the first and second person agree with their nominatives in number and person; as, بَنْ كُورْدُمْ (bèn gyûrdûm) *I saw, have seen* (him, her, it, &c.) ; سِزْ كُورْدُيكُزْ (sĭz gyûrdûnûz) *you saw, have seen* (me, us, them, &c.).

A verb of the third person must also agree with its subject, if *understood;* as, كُورْدِى (gyûrdû) *he, she, it saw, has seen* (it,&c.); كُورْدُيلَرْ (gyûrdûlèr) *they saw, have seen* (it, &c.).

When the subject is *expressed* of a verb of the third person, the verb does not always agree with it in number. A singular subject sometimes has its verb in the plural, out of respect or politeness ; a plural subject often has its verb in the singular, so as to avoid the cacophony of repetition.   Thus : بَابَامْ كِتْدِيلَرْ

(bábäm gïtdïlér) *my father went, has gone, is gone* ; اوشَاقْلَرى كَلْدى
(úshäqlérï gáldï) *his* or *their servants came,* or *have come, are
come.*

So a verb with several subjects expressed, when all of the
third person, singular or plural, may be in the singular ; as,
اُلُوفِ رِضْوَانْ و صُنُوفِ غُفْرَانْ شَايَانْ دِرْ (álüf-ï rïzvän ú súnüf-ï gúfrän
shäyän dïr) *thousands of prayers for God's acceptance, and all
kinds of wishes for God's mercy* (on him, &c.) *is* (are) *fitting.*

· If one of them be of the second person, singular or plural,
and the other or others of the third person, the verb must be
of the second person plural ; as, سَنْ وَ پَدَرِمْ وَ قُوكْشِيكُزْ بَرَابَرْ كِتْدِيكِزْ
(sän vé pédérïm vé qóñshúñúz béräbér gïtdïñïz) *thou and my
father, with your neighbour, went together.*

And if one be of the first person, even singular, whether the
others be of the second or third, singular or plural, the verb
must be in the first person plural ; as, بَنْ وَ سَنْ وَ قَرِنْدَاشِكْ كُورْدُكْ
(bén, vé sän, vé qárndäshïñ, gyúrdúk) *I, and thou, and thy
brother, saw* (him, &c.).

In conversation, دِرْ and its plural دِرْلَرْ are generally omitted
at the end of a phrase, affirmative, negative, or interrogative ;
as, كَيْفِكُزْ اِيُو مِى (kéyfïñïz ïyï mï) *is your health good ?* اِيُو (ïyï)
it is good; اِيُو دِكِلْ (ïyï dïyïl) *it is not good.*

But, in repeating the affirmative or negative words of
another, دِرْ must be introduced ; as, بُويْلَه دِرْ دَيُو تَصْدِيقْ اَيْلَدى

(bûylè dîr, dèyû, tâsdîq èylèdî) *he confirmed, saying, " It is so."*

In relating the words of another, no alteration is permitted in number, person, or tense of the verb; as, گلورم دیدی (gèlîrîm, dîdî) *he said, " I will come"* (not as in English, *" he said he would come"*).

When the object of a transitive verb is definite, it is put in the accusative; as, آتی آلدم (âtî âldîm) *I bought, have bought (or taken) the horse.* But, if the object be indefinite, it remains in the nominative; as, آت آلدم (ât âldûn) *I bought a horse* or *horses.*

Intransitive, like transitive, verbs, govern their indirect objects by means of different prepositions, *i.e.*, the substantives or pronouns are put into different cases according to the verb. Thus : اولومدن قورقمق (ûlûmdûn qòrqmâq) *to be afraid of death ;* اولومدن قاچمق (ûlûmdûn qâchmâq) *to run away from death;* پاره‌یه باقمق (pârâyâ bâqmâq) *to look at money (i.e.,* to take money into account or consideration); صویه یوزمك (sûdâ yûzmèk) *to swim in the water;* دكزه كیرمك (dènîzè gîrmèk) *to go into the sea (i.e.,* to bathe in the sea); قلج ایله اورمق (qîllj ìlâ wûrmâq) *to strike with a (or the) sword ;* خاطر ایچون یاپمق (khātîr ìchîn yâpmâq) *to do (a thing) out of regard* (for some one); حیوانه بنمك (hâywânâ bînmèk) *to mount on a beast* (horse);

كـــمىيَه بِنمَكْ (gėmlyė bìnmėk) *to mount* (go) *on board ship;*

آيَاغَه قَـالقَمَقْ (áyághá qálqmáq) *to rise to one's feet* (i.e., *to rise, get up, stand up).*

Nouns of time and place are often used adverbially (as also is the case in English) without prepositions after verbs; as, يَارِينْ كَلْ (yārìn gál) *come to-morrow;* آشَاغِى اِينْ (áshághì ìn, *vulg.* èn) *descend, come or go down;* يُوقَارِى چِقْ (yùqárì chìq) *ascend, mount;* i.e., *come or go up.* Still, on occasions, prepositions are used with them; as, صَاغَه صَاپْ (sághá sáp) *deviate* (turn) *to the right;* صُولَه بَاقْ (sòlá báq) *look to the left;* كِـيرُو كِيتْ (gìrù, *vulg.* gèrì gìt) *go back;* كِـيرُودَنْ كَلْ (gèrìdán gál) *come from the rear, from behind.*

A transitive verb has sometimes two direct objects, one definite, the other indefinite; as, آنِى مُشِيرْ اِتْدِيلَرْ (ánì mùshīr ėtdìlėr) *they made him a* mushīr (duke, or field-marshal).

An Ottoman compound verb, active or passive, often takes its direct or indirect object into the body of the verb, as the Persian complement of its nominal factor; as, بُو دَقِيقَيَه تَحْصِيلِ وُقُوفْ أَيْلَدِى (bù dáqìqáyá táhsīlì vwùqūf ėylėdì) *he acquired cognizance of* (about) *this subtle point;* صَرْفِ مُزْجَاتِ بِضَاعَه قِيلِنْدِى (sárf-ì mùzjāt-ì bìzā'á qìlìndì) *expenditure of the* modicum *of capital was made* (i.e., *the* modicum *of capital was spent).*

N

Section VII. *Syntax of the Participle.*

In conversation, the substantive qualified by a particle, active or passive, is sometimes understood, and the participle is used as a substantive; as, گلَنَه ویر (gèlánè vèr) *give* (thou it) *to him* (or *her*) *who comes* ; کیدیکمَ باقمَ (gìdìyìmâ bâqmâ) *look not at that which I wear* ; یاپه جغمی صورمَ (yâpâjâghìmì sòrmâ) *ask not what I shall do.*

The active participle present of اُولمَق, i. e. اُولان, is often omitted after Arabic participles, active or passive ; as, رُبع مسکونده واقع مَمَالك و بلدان (rûb'ì mèskyûndâ vwâqï' mèmālìk ù bûldān) *the countries and towns situated in the inhabited quarter* (of the globe); بو کتابده مذکور فنون ومعارف (bû kìtâbdâ mèz-kyûr fûnūn ù mâ'ärìf) *the sciences and matters of knowledge mentioned in this book.*

Active participles govern all their objects in the same way as the verbs from which they derive ; so also do the passive participles, excepting only the object they each qualify as an adjective ; as, قَپُو آچَان (qâpù âchân) *he who opens a door ;* قَپویی آچَان (qâpùyù âchân) *he who* (*that which*) *opens the door ;* اَلِم ایلَه آچدیغم قَپُو (èlìm ìlè âchdìghìm qâpù) *the door that I opened with my hand ;* پدریمك بونی قَبُول ایدَمَیَجَکی سَبَب (pèdèrì-mìñ bùnù qâbūl ìdèmèyèjèyì sèbèb) *the reason for which my father will not be able to accept this.*

The Persian and Arabic participles are constructed, generally, with their objects, in the same manner as if the participles were substantives; as, خَالِقِ هَرْدُوجِهَانْ (khāllq-î hėr dû jIhāu), هَرْ دُو جِهَانِكْ خَالِقِى (hėr dû jIhānîñ khāllqî) *the Creator of both worlds;* مَخْلُوقِ يَـدِ قُـدْرَتِى (mâkhlūq-û yėd-i qûdrėtl), يَـدِ قُدْرَتْلَرِنِكْ مَخْلُوقِى (yėd-i qûdrėtlėrlnlñ mâkhlūqû) *the creature of the hand of His almighty power;* آفَرِينَنْدَهِ اِينُ وَ آنْ (āfėrinėndė-l în û ān) *the Creator of this and that* (all things); چَرْخِ اَثِيرْ رَسِيدَهِ كُنْكُرَهِ (rėsîdė-l kyûngyûrė-'l chârkh-î ėsîr) *which has reached the battlement of the ethereal sphere.*

But sometimes Arabic active participles of transitive verbs govern their direct objects as do their verbs; thus, كَيْفِيَّتِ مَذْكُورَهِى مُبِينْ (kėyfIyyėt-l mėzkyûrė-l mûbîn) *which explains the said circumstance.*

SECTION VIII. *Syntax of the Verbal Nouns and Infinitive.*

Turkish verbal nouns are constructed with their subjects, when substantives, as any two substantives; thus, اَحْمَدِكْ كَلْمَسِى (âhmėdlñ gâlmėsl) *the coming of Ahmed, Ahmed's coming;* اَحْمَدِكْ كَلْدِيكِى (âhmėdlñ gâldlyl) *Ahmed's* (past action of) *having come;* اَحْمَدِكْ كَلَجَكِى (âhmėdlñ gėlėjėyl) *Ahmed's* (future action of) *coming.*

When the subject is a pronoun, it is put in the genitive still, and the Turkish verbal noun takes the possessive suffix of the subject's number and person ; as, بَنِمْ كَلَمَمْ (bĕnĭm gălmĕm) *my coming* ; سَنِكْ كَلْدِيكِكْ (sălน găldĭyĭñ) *thy having come* ; كَلَجَكَّرِى اَنْـلَـرِكْ (ănlĕrĭñ gălĕjĕklĕrĭ) *their future coming.*

Turkish verbal nouns and infinitives are constructed with their objects, direct or indirect, exactly as their verbs ; thus, اَنِى كُورْمَمْ (ănĭ gyŭrmĕm) *my seeing him (her, it)* ; اِزْمِيرَه كَلَجَكِكْ (Izmĭrĕ gălĕjĕyĭñ) *thy future coming to Smyrna* ; دُونْ مَكْتُوبْ يَازْدِيغِى پَدَرِنَه اَحْمَدِكْ (pĕdĕrĭnă ăhmĕdĭñ dŭn mĕktūb yăzdĭghĭ) *Ahmed's having written a letter to his father yesterday.*

Arabic verbal nouns are constructed with their agents sometimes in the Turkish, sometimes in the Arabic, and sometimes in the Persian manner ; as, وُرُودُمْ (vŭrūdŭm) *my arrival* ; تَحْصِيلِكْ (tăhsīlĭñ) *thy study* ; تَحْرِيرِى (tăhrīrĭ) *his writing* ; صُنْعِ اللّٰه (sŭn'ŭ 'llāh), صُنْعِ الِلّٰهْ (sŭn'-ĭ llāh) *the act of God* ; اِدَارَهٔ پَرْكَارِ اَفْكَارْ (Idārĕ-ĭ pĕrgyār-ĭ ĕfkyār) *a revolving of the compasses of the thoughts.*

Arabic verbal nouns are constructed with their objects in the same manner as the compound verbs formed of them ; as, مَقْدُورِى صَرْفْ فَنّ (măqdŭrĭ sărf) *an employing one's utmost* ; جَغْرَافِيَابِى تَحْصِيلَه مَدَارْ (fănn-ĭ jăgrāfĭyăyĭ tăhsĭlă mĕdār) *a help to an acquiring the science of geography.* But they may also be constructed with them as two simple substantives, either in the Turkish or Persian manner ; as, صَرْفِى مَقْدُورَكْ or مَقْدُورْ صَرْفِ ;

and again, تَحْصِيلِنَه جَغْرَافْيَانِكْ or جَغْرَافْيَايَه فَنِّ تَحْصِيلِ فَنِّ ; &c.

In all cases excepting their construction with their subjects or objects, the Turkish verbal nouns and infinitives are constructed in sentences exactly like any other substantives ; as, دِرْ اَوْلَى بُونْدَنْ اُولْمَكْ (ûlmék bûndân êvlâ dîr) *to die is better than this* ; جَالِشْدِى قُورْتُلْمَغَه (qûrtûlmâghâ châlîshdî) *he laboured at escaping* ; اِتْدِمْ تَرْتِيب اِيچُون يَاقْمَق (yâqmâq ichîn têrtîb êtdîm) *I arranged, have arranged* (it) *for burning* ; دِكِلْ لَازِمْ كَلْمَسِى (gâl-mésî lâzîm dîyîl) *his coming* (is) *not necessary* ; كِيدَبِيلَجَكِمَه (gidê-bîlêjêyîmê shûb-hêm vâr) *my doubt exists*, i. e., *I have a doubt as to my being able to go*.

SECTION IX. *Syntax of the Gerunds.*

The gerunds are not much used in conversation ; there the discourse is broken up into as many sentences as may be needed, each with its personal verb ; as, كِتْدِمْ كُورْدُمْ كَلْدِمْ خَبَرْ وِيرْدِمْ (gitdîm, gyûrdûm, gâldîm, khâbêr vêrdîm) *I went ; I saw ; I came ; I gave information.*

But, in the literary style, one long phrase, ending with one personal verb, will contain a number of clauses, each ending with a gerund (which thus acts to the ear, as well as to the eye, like our commas and semicolons) ; as, كِيدُوبْ كُورُوبْ كَلْدِكْدَه

خَبَرْ وِيرْدُمْ (gïdŭp, gyŭrèrek, gĕldïkdĕ, khŭbèr vèrdïm), *I, going and seeing, on coming back, reported.*

When compound verbs are used, the auxiliary gerunds may be omitted once or twice in a long sentence ; as, بِرْ مَوْضِعَه وُرُودْ وَ أَنْدَه بِرْ مِقْدَارْ قُعُودْ اِيدُوبْ (bïr mèvzï'â vŭrūd, vè ândâ bïr mïqdār qu'ūd èdŭp, ...) ... *arriving at a certain place, and sitting down there awhile,* .... In this case, however, a conjunction requires to be introduced in lieu of the gerund omitted ; as is seen in the example given.

The subjects, and direct or indirect objects, of the gerunds are constructed as with their verbs. But, as the gerunds cannot indicate the person and number of their subjects, the appropriate personal pronoun must be expressed before them, when the subject is not a substantive ; as, آدَمْ كِتَابْ أُوقُويُوبْ (âdâm kïtāb ôqŭyŭb) *man, reading a book* (or *books*), ...;

فَرْمَانِمْ سِزَه وَاصِلْ أُولِيجَقْ (fèrmānïm sïzè vwāsïl ôlïjâq) *at what time my command shall attain unto you,* ......; بَنْ شُو آدَمِى كُورَرَكْ (bèn, shŭ âdâmï gyŭrèrèk) *I, seeing that man,* ......; &c.

SECTION X. *Syntax of the Adverb.*

The adverb precedes the verb or adjective qualified by it ; as, صَبَاحْلَيِنْ كَلْدِى (sâbāhlèyïn gĕldï) *he came in the morning;* جُوقْ كُوزَلْ (chôq gyŭzèl) *very pretty.*

The negative دكِل (dîyîl) *not*, precedes the verb substantive, expressed or understood, but follows the substantive or adjective which it negatives; as, كَـنْـج دِيِّـلِـم (génj dîyîlîm) *I am not young*; عَقْلْـسِزْ دِيْلِسِـن (åqlsîz dîyîlsîn) *thou art not unintelligent*; آدَمْ دِكِل دِرْ (ådåm dîyîl dîr) *he or it is not a man*; &c.

The adverbial suffixes دَك (dèk), دَكِين (dèyîn), follow a noun of time, place, or condition, in the dative; as, صَبَاحَ دَكِين (såbåhå dèyîn) *until morning*; لُوَنْدُرَيَدَك (lóndúråyådèk) *as far as London*; أُوْلُوَمَدَك (ålúmèdèk) *until death*. They follow the third gerund also, put in this same dative case, and thus form a verbal limit of time; as, كَلَنْجَـيَـدَك (gèlînjèyèdèk) *until* (I, thou, &c.) *come, came*. The agent must be named or understood; as, بَنْ كِدِنْجَـيَـدَك (bèn gîdînjèyèdèk) *until I go* (or *went*); مَـكْـتُوبُم أُورَايَـه وَارِنْجَـيَـدَك (mèktúbûm óråyå vårînjåyådèk) *until my letter reach* (or *reached*) *there*. The tense of this gerund is decided by the context, in like manner as its agent and object.

The adverb كُـوْرَه (gyûrè) *according*, also follows a dative; as, عَقْلِمَه كُـوْرَه ('åqlîmå gyûrè) *according to my judgment*; بَكَا كُـوْرَه (bånå gyûrè) *according to me*; &c.

The adverbs يَكَا (yånå), طُوَلَايِى (dólåyî), أُوَتُورُى (åtúrú) *relatively*, follow substantives or infinitives in the ablative; as, كِـتَابَدَن طُوَلَايِى (kîtåbdån dólåyî) *relatively to* (about) *a* (or *the*) *book ;* كِتْمَكْدَنْ اُوتُورُى (gïtmékdån ûtûrû) *relatively to* (about, concerning) *going.*

Although it is not grammatically erroneous, in answering a question, to use the affirmative adverb اَوَتْ (évét) or بَلِى (bélï) *yes,* or the negative يُوقْ (yôq) or خَيْر (khåyr) *no,* when appropriate, it is unidiomatic to do so. The more general custom, whether one of those adverbs be used or not, is to repeat the word or words of the question on which the interrogation turns, with such grammatical modifications as may be necessary. Thus, turning back to the five questions instanced in Chap. II., sect. 21 (p. 151-2), the respective answers may be : 1, اَوَتْ بَنْ (évét, bén) *yes, I* (am to ride); 2, يُوقْ اُولَبِرْكُونْ (yôq, ôlbïr gyûn) *no, the day after; &c.*

SECTION XI. *Syntax of the Preposition.*

The Turkish preposition always follows the word it governs, noun, pronoun, or verbal derivative, as is seen in Chap. II., sections 1 (p. 51), 4 (p. 82), 5 (p. 83), 6 (p. 89), 7 (p. 90), and in Chap. III., section 8 (p. 179) ; but the Arabic and Persian prepositions always precede ; as, عَلَى التَّحْقِيقْ ('ålé 't-tåhqïq) *in truth ;* بِرْ قَرَارْ (bér qårår) *in permanence* (without change); عَلَيْحِدَه ('ålå hïdé) *singly ;* فِى الْوَاقِعْ (fï 'l-wåqï') *in fact ;* عَلَى كَلَا التَّقْدِيرَيْن ('ålå bï-éyyï hålïn) *in any case ;* بِأَيِّ حَالٍ ('ålå kélá 't-táqdiiéyn) *upon either supposition ;* اَزْ سَرِ نَو (éz sér-i név) *from a new beginning* (over again, again).

A preposition may govern two or more substantives in a sentence ; as, اَلْ وَاَصْحَابُ وَعِتْرَتُ وَاَحْبَايِنَه *to his family, companions, posterity, and friends.*

But, as the Arabic and Persian preposition precedes the adjectives that qualify, as well as the substantives qualified, so the Turkish preposition is placed after all these ; consequently, in Persian construction, and when the substantive is followed by the possessive suffixes, the Turkish preposition is separated from the substantive it governs, sometimes by a considerable distance ; as, بَابَامْ ايلَه (bábá-m ilé) *with my father ;* بُو مُحِبّ صَادِقْدَه (bú múhibb-i sádiq-dá) *in this faithful friend ;* قَالْيُونِ كُوَه نُمُونِ هُمَايُونُكْ بَاشِى (qáliyún-i kyúh-námún-i húmáyúnúñ báshí) *the head of the mountain-like imperial galley.*

SECTION XII. *Syntax of the Conjunction.*

All conjunctions, except the enclitic دَه (dé, dá), or دَخِى (dákhí), *too, also,* head the phrase they belong to.

The enclitic conversational دَه, or literary دَخِى, is placed after the word of a phrase to which special attention is directed ; thus : اِسْتَانْبُولْدَنْ دَخِى طُوبْ گَلْدِى (istánbóldán dákhí, or istánbóddándá tóp gáldí) *cannon came from Constantinople also ;* اِسْتَانْبُولْدَنْ طُوبْ

دَخِی كُلْدِی (Istàubòldàn tòp dàkhì gàldì) *cannon, too, came from Constantinople.*

This enclitic is repeated after each member of a phrase linked together by its use; as, بَنْدَه كِيدَرِمْ سَنْدَه (bèn-dà gèdèrìm; sàn-dà) *I, too, will go, as also thou;* بَنْدَه سَنْدَه أُولْدَه أُوجُمُزْ كِيدَرِزْ (bèn-dà, sàn-dà, ò-dà, ùchùmùz gìdèrìz) *I, thou, and he too, will all three go.*

It is often placed after a verb in the conditional, its sense being then, in English, rendered by *even;* as, كَلْسَهدَه (gàlsè-dè) *even should he come;* كَلْمِشْ ایسَهدَه (gàlmìsh ìsè-dè) *even though he be come;* كَلْسَیْدِیدَه (gàlsèydì-dà) *had he even come;* كَلَجَكْ أُولْسَهدَه (gàlèjèk òlsà-dà) *even should he be about to come* (even should he think of coming, or resolve to come).

After other verbs than conditionals, it is enclitic with each that enters a phrase, and answers to our *both,* followed by *and* or *also;* as, كِلُورِمْدَه كُورُرُمْدَه (gèllrìm-dà, gyùrùrùm-dà) *I will both come, and see also;* — , — ,) كِلُورِمْدَه كُورُرُمْدَه بَكِنُورْ ایسَهمْ آلُورِمْدَه bèyànìr-ìsè-m, àlìrìm-dà) *I will come, and I will see, and if I admire, will also buy.*

The conjunctions اِسْتَرْ, كَرَكْ, هَا, in the sense of *whether ...,* or *whether,* أَكَرْ (èyèr) *if,* with كَرْجِه (gèr-chì, *vulg.* gèrchè) or أَكَرْجِه (èyèr-chì, *vulg.* egèrchè) *although,* put the verb or verbs of their phrase in the conditional; as, هَاكَلْسَه هَاكَلْمَسَه (hà gàlsè,

há gálmásá) *whether he come, or* (whether he come) *not;* اَكَرْكُلْسَه
(éyér gálsá) *if he come;* اَكَرْجِه كُلْمِشْ اِيَسَدَه (égérchí gálmísh ísá-
dá) *although he be even come* (even though he be come).

When the copulative و joins one verb or phrase to another,
it is pronounced vé, in conformity (to a certain degree) with
its original Arabic pronunciation; but when, in Persian construction, it unites two nouns, substantive or adjective, it takes
the vowel-sound of ŭ or ú, and joins on, in pronunciation, as
though in a syllable, with the consonant preceding it; as,
دَوْلَتْ وَ اِقْبَالْ كَلْدِى وَ كُوْرْدِى (gáldí vé gyŭrdú) *he came, and he saw;*
(dévlét ú íqbāl) *fortune and prosperity;* قَوِى وَ تَنْدُرُسْتْ (qávī-yú
tén-dŭrŭst) *strong and healthy.*

The Persian conjunction كِ (kí) *that,* always connects two
members of a phrase, and should never be supposed to be a
relative pronoun in Turkish (as it really is in Persian, as well
as a conjunction); as, مَعْلُومْ اُولَه كِه (má'lūm ólá kí) *be it known
that* .... Sometimes the clause that follows shows the cause
or reason of that which precedes; the conjunction may then
be rendered by *for* or *because;* as, نِيَازْمَنْدْ اُولَهلِمْ وَ نَالَه كُنَانْ كِه جِنْسِ
مَغْفَرَتَه سِيمِ اَشْكْ اُولْدِى نُقُودْ (níyāzménd ólálím, vé nālé-kyŭnān, kí
jíns-í mágférété sīm-í éshk óldú núqūd) *let us be instant in sup-
plications, and assiduous in moans, for the silver of* (man's) *tears
has been made the coins payable for the wares of* (God's) *mercy.*
(The inversion نُقُودْ اُولْدِى for اُولْدِى نُقُودْ is poetical.)

After a verb signifying *to say* (which also may mean, *to say to one's self, to think*), or *to ask*, the conjunction كه introduces, what is, was, or will be said or thought; but the question must be in the mood, tense, number, and person, in the very words, used by the speaker or thinker; as, دِيُورْكِه يَارِينْ گُلُورِمْ (dìyòr kì, yārìn gèlìrìm) *he says, I will come to-morrow*; صُوزْدِى كِـه بُو نَه دِرْ (sòrdù kì, bù nè dìr) *he asked, What is this?* We see, then, that كه, so used, is the equivalent of our sign of quotation, the *inverted commas.* We cannot alter the phrase as is our custom, and say, *he says he will come,* or *he asked what that was.*

Occasionally, in a certain style, this كه is omitted; as, دِيدِى أَىْ شَهْرِيَارْ (dìdì: èy shèhrìyār) *he exclaimed, "O monarch."*

But the method more generally used, especially in conversation, and which is the true Turkish mode, is to quote first what was said, asked, or thought, and then immediately to bring in the verb *to say, &c.,* in its proper tense, number, and person; as, گُلُورِزْ دِيُورْلَرْ (gèlìrìz dìyòrlèr) *they say, We will come;* i. e., *they say they will come;* كُورْمَدِمْ دِيدِى (gyùrmàdìm dìdì) *he said, I did not see* (him, her, it, them, you, &c.); i. e., *he said he did not see.* In this case, if the verb used be any other than دِيمَكْ, the Turkish conjunction دِيُو (dìyù, *vulg.* dèyè), which really is the first or fifth gerund, modified by usage, of دِيمَكْ, *viz.,* دِيُوبْ or دِيَه, is introduced before the verb used, and after the quotation; it is the equivalent of our *saying;* as, كَـيْفِكَـزْ ايومِى دِيُو

سُؤَالْ اِيتْـدِمْ (kéyfîñîz íyî-mî, diyú, sûᵓāl étdîm) *I asked* (of him or her), *saying, Is your health yood ?* i. e., *I asked how he was;*

بِلْمَيُورُزْ دِيُو اِنْكَارْ اِيدِيُورْلَرْ (bélméyórîz, diyú, înkyār ídîyórlér) *they deny, saying, We know not;* i. e., *they deny, and say they know not;* كَلْمَزْسِكِزْ دِيُو خُولْيَا اِيتْدِمْ (gálmázsîñîz, diyú, khúlyá étdîm) *I formed an idea, saying* (to myself), *You will not come;* i. e., *I imagined that you would not come;* نَه دِيُو كَلْدِيكِزْ (né diyú, gál-dîñîz) *saying what* (to thyself), *art thou come?* i. e., *what are you come for?*

The conjunction كِه sometimes, as in Persian, serves to connect an incidental qualifying phrase to an antecedent noun, as though it were a relative pronoun; but in such case it never undergoes declension or takes a preposition, the following phrase being complete in all its parts; as, حَمْدُ و سِپَاسْ اُولْ

خُدَاوَنْدِ بِى عِلَّتَه سَزَا دِرْكِه وُجُودِ اَنْهَارُ وقُعُورِ بِحَارْ يَكْقَطْرَه‌ءِ قُدْرَتِ نَامُتَنَاهِلَرِى دِرْ

(hámd ú sîpās ól khúdāvénd-î bī-ᵓîllété sézā dîr, kî, vújūd-î énhār ú qúᵓūr-î bîhār yék-qátré-î qúdrét-î nā-múténāhîlérî dîr) *glory and lauds are worthy of that uncaused Lord God, of whose infinite power the existence of rivers and the depths of oceans are but a single drop.*

The foregoing example shows that it is often difficult or impossible to distinguish whether the phrase that follows كِه is a qualificative, or the exposition of a reason. We might take it in this latter sense, and translate: *for, the existence of rivers, &c., are but one drop, &c.*

But, in ethical works and the like, generally composed by members of the 'ûlêmā class (Doctors of Canon Law) on a Persian or Arabic model, the clause that follows كِه is generally qualificative, and the style is anti-Turkish. Thus : هَرْكَسْ كِه

دَسْتِ هِمَّتْ اِيـلَه حَبْلِ مَتِينِ عَقْلَه مُتَشَبِّثْ أُولَه (hèr kès kî dèst-i hîmmèt ilâ hâbl-i mêtîn-i 'âqlâ mâtêshêbbîs ôlâ, ...); *every one who shall take hold of the firm cable of reason with the hand of endeavour, ...; بُو جَانْوَرْلَرْكِه نَظَرِ عِبْرَتْلَه مَنْظُورْ دِرْ (bû jānvèrlèr kî nâzâr-i 'îbrêt-lâ mânzûr dûr, ...) these animals which are looked upon with a regard for instruction, ...*

The conjunctions تَا كِه (tā kî) *in order that,* شَايَدْ كِه (shāyèd kî) *perhaps, lest,* مَدَامْكِه (mâ-dām-kî) *as long as, since,* مَبَادَا كِه (mê-bādā kî) *lest,* مَگَرْ كِه (mèyèr kî) *unless,* require their verbs to be in the optative; as, تَا كِه تَحَمُّلِى قَالْمَيَه (— — tâhâmmûlû qâlmâyâ) *in order that no power of endurance be left in him;* شَايَدْ كِه مُنْهَزِمْ أُولَلَرْ (— — mûnhèzîm ôlâlèr) *lest they be routed;* مَادَامْكِه حَيَاتْدَه اُولَلَرْ (—— hâyâtdâ ôlâlèr) *since they are alive;* مَگَرْ كِه كُوزَلْ أُولَه (— — ûylè ôlâ) *lest it be so;* مَبَادَا كِه أُويْـلَه أُولَه (— — gyûzèl ôlâ) *unless he (she, it) be beautiful.*

SECTION XIII. *Syntax of the Interjection.*

Some interjections are accompanied by nouns and pronouns, some by nouns only, others have no accompaniment, and some precede verbs.

When accompanied by a noun, the noun is always in the nominative, excepting with the interjection يَازِق (yázîq) ; as, وَاخْ بَابَامْ (vwākh bâbâm) *alas, my father!* آفَرِين اُوغْلُمْ (āfèrìn, *vulg.* āfèrìm òghlûm) *well done, my boy!* كِيدِى أَدَبْسِزْ (gìdì édèb-siz) *O, impudent fellow!* آى قَرِنْدَاشِمْ (èy qârdâshìm) *well, brother!* مَرْحَبَا أَفَنْدِمْ (mèrhâbâ èfèndìm) *God's blessing on you, sir!* آمَانْ جُوجُغُمْ (âmân chòjûghûm) *O, my child!* They always precede the noun. The word يَازِق is used in this way also, but it further permits its substantive to be put in the dative; as, يَا:ِق أَمَكِمْ (yāzìq èmèyìm), يَازِق أَمَكِمَ (yāzìq èmèyìmè) *alas my trouble! alas for my trouble!*

When accompanied by a pronoun, except the interjection كِيدِى (gìdì), the pronoun must be in the dative; as, يَازِق بَكَا (yázîq bâñâ) *poor me!* وَاخْ سَكَا (vwākh sâñâ) *alas for thee!* آفَرِين أَنْلَرَه (āfèrìm ânlârâ) *well done, they!* The exceptional كِيدِى is constructed with the accusative of the second person singular, which it may precede or follow; as, كِيدِى سَنِى (gìdì sânì) or سَنِى كِيدِى (sânì gìdì) *faugh, thou (good-for-nothing)!*

Interjections indicative of a desire for the future or regret for the past, are constructed with the conditional, aorist or past accordingly; as, آه كلسه (āh gålså) *O that he would come!* آه كلسیدی (āh gålseydĭ) *O that he had come!* One of these, آمان, is constructed also with the imperative, and expresses vehement desire with the affirmative, or dread with the negative; as, آمان كتمسه (āmån gĭtmåså) *O that he go not* (by his own desire)! آمان كتمسین (āmån gĭtmåsĭn) *O that he go not* (if my wish prevail)!

With an imperative, هله (hėlė) expresses an invitation or a challenge; as, هله كل (hėlė gål) *come along!* هله كلسون (hėlė gålsĭn) *just let him only come!*

Arabic phrases are often used as interjections, generally after proper names; as, مكّه مكرّمه كرّمها الله تعالی (mėkkė-ĭ mükėrrėmė, kėrrėmå-hå 'llåhŭ tåālå) *Mekka the Venerated, which may God, who be exalted, cause to be venerated!* سلطان غازی سلیم خان مدّ الله ظلال رأفته علی مفارق الانام ما تكرّر الشهور و تجدّد الاعوام حضرتلری *His Majesty, the champion of the faith, Sultan Selim Khan, the shadows of whose clemency may God spread over the crowns of the heads of mankind, so long as the months repeat themselves and the years renew themselves!*

FINIS.

ADDENDUM.

In p. 45, after line 5, as a further remark on the uses of letter و , the following rule is not without its use; viz.,—

In a few words of Persian origin only, the letter و , following a letter خ , and itself followed by a long vowel-letter ا , is suppressed and lost in the pronunciation. Thus خوان kh'ān, خواه kh'āh, خواهش kh'āhīsh. The word خواجه kh'ājā, of this class, and its derivatives, خواجگان , خواجهلِق , &c., have been corrupted in Turkish into khójá, khójágyān, khójálíq, &c. In Persian proper, a very few words beginning with خو , without a following ا , elide the و in like manner in pronouncing; but this is never observed in Turkish, unless it may be in the rhyme-words of ancient poetry. Thus the word خوش (usually read khūsh in Persian, khósh in Turkish) is made to rhyme with وش vésh, for instance; and in consequence must then be read kh'āsh. خود (usually khūd, Turkish khód) is made to rhyme with بد béd; something after the manner of our poets, who make *wind* rhyme with *find*, *mind*, &c. This is what is styled واو معدوله (vwāwí má'dūlè), *deflected* و , in Persian.

INDEX.

A.

London: Gilbert & Rivington, Limited, St. John's Sq., Clerkenwell Road.

www.ingramcontent.com/pod-product-compliance
Lightning Source LLC
Chambersburg PA
CBHW030822270326
41928CB00007B/854